CAMPING TIPS FOR THE BEST CAMPING TRIPS

By John McDonald

WMI
BOOKS

Camping Tips for Best Camping Trips

ISBN: 0-97367071-1

Published by WMI Books
161 Frederick Street, Suite 200
Toronto, Ontario M5A 4P3 Canada

Distributed in Canada by
Canadian Book Network
c/o Georgetown Terminal Warehouses
34 Armstrong Avenue
Georgetown, Ontario L7G 4R9
www.canadianbooknetwork.com

Distributed in the United States by
CDS
193 Edwards Drive
Jackson TN 38301
www.cdsbooks.com

Printed and bound in Canada

Contents

 # Introduction to Camping

Growing up in the city may have added to the mystery and enchantment of camping, but it will always be one of my greatest and most vivid childhood memories. Packing up the car with the gear and gadgets I was only permitted to use when camping, the sleeping bags still infused with the scent of past campfires, and the old steel-belted Coleman cooler that resembled an old war relic, proudly wearing battle wounds from raccoons and even worse critters, like my brothers and me.

For most of us, camping was an exciting summer tradition that would bring the family together in a way that could only happen in the great outdoors. No television or similar distractions around for miles, just you and your family spending time together cooking, cleaning, fishing, swimming, hiking, and a myriad of other activities, all packed into one fun-filled week.

Everything was done together, and nothing seemed like a chore. You wanted to help cook, build a fire, and clean the camp site before you retired to your tent for the night. Going back to the basics somehow puts everything into perspective; just like when the power goes out for a few hours and you have to use candles and actually talk to each other. It is these special rare moments that we could all use more of in today's world, in my opinion.

I remember roasting marshmallows and cooking spider-cut hot dogs over the campfire, searching for the perfect stick and carving the end with my pocket knife, staring up at the star-filled sky at night, which was much more spectacular away from the city. Memories like these and a thousand others are what make camping so special.

Jump ahead to over 20 years later, and I now work in the camping industry, heading the marketing and communications department for North America's largest camping reservation service. Working here at

ReserveAmerica has been a rewarding experience, as I can relive my memories each day as I think of ways to improve the trip-planning experience for the millions of customers that use our service each year. I have created camping magazines, a camping credit card, the largest camping e-mail newsletter in the industry, and even built the "World's Largest S'more" to kick-off the camping season—100 feet long by 16 feet wide, weighing in at 1,600 pounds and made with 7,000 chocolate bars, 20,000 marshmallows and 24,000 graham crackers. Where else would you get to build a 1,600-pound s'more? Try asking your boss if you can do the same and see what the response may be!

This book, *Camping Tips for the Best Camping Trips,* was created out of the tremendous response we have received from our monthly newsletter and our customers. Many moons ago, against the advice of many people, I pushed for and deployed the first e-mail newsletter to our customers. This e-mail was sent to roughly 200,000 customers and I sat at the edge of my seat all morning waiting to hit the "send" button. Were people going to be upset that we were e-mailing them? Did we pick the right content to include? Recipes, gear reviews, park spotlights, song sheets, kid's games, and campfire stories—what was I thinking?

All of the stress and tension almost immediately vanished as people started sending in their responses. Just minutes after it was released, customers sent in great feedback about the newsletter and provided tips and recipes of their own to consider for future issues. Customers would even write after a camping trip to tell us they made the recipe or brought our song sheets with them to the park and what a great time they had. Growing to well over a million subscribers currently, our newsletter continues to receive great feedback and we continually work to improve it each issue based on the guidance of our customers' needs.

This book has been crafted to help continually serve the needs of our customers and to help plan their camping trip and make it a more enjoyable experience. I truly hope that this book becomes a keepsake for your family, and that you go back to it each time you plan your next outdoor adventure. It is certainly a special feeling to know that creating and developing all of these programs for our customers has been both appreciated and utilized.

Let's go camping!
John McDonald

Chapter 1:
Top Secrets of
Camping

CAMPING TIPS

Here is a collection of tips that should help ensure an enjoyable trip. One tip you should definitely follow: Before you head out on your camping adventure be sure to let someone know of your destination plans and how long you expect to be gone.

Camping Etiquette Checklist

Most campers drive for hours and plan far in advance for their camping trips to our beautiful parks and campgrounds. Some of the reasons for going camping are to get away from it all, and spend time with our families breathing the fresh air and taking in the beautiful surroundings. That is why it can be very disappointing to finally arrive at the campground only to have people at other camp sites making your trip hard to enjoy. If we all follow these simple guidelines, everyone at the park should be able to have a great camping trip.

1. *Do not walk through other camp sites.* Even if it would make it easier to get to washrooms or other park locations, walking through another person's camp site is very intrusive and many people will find this offensive.

2. *Keep your pet on a leash at all times.* It can be a nuisance to have other pets on your camp site when you are trying to relax. Even though you may not feel it is a big deal, not everyone wants your dog running through their camp site.

3. *Pick up after your dog.* Nothing spoils a walk more than stepping in dog-do (especially with bare feet!). Bring a scoop or plastic bags to pick up and dispose of pet waste properly. Special bags can be found at pet supply stores or even the "dollar" store (some camp stores carry them as well).

4. *Always fully extinguish your campfire before sleeping or leaving your camp site.* Not only is it dangerous and against most park regulations to leave a fire smouldering, but the smoke can become overwhelming when a campfire is not maintained properly.

5. *Be thoughtful when using a radio.* Observe quiet hours or radio-free zones and take the time to ask if the radio is too loud for your camp site neighbors.

6. *Minimize noise around the campfire late at night.* Although everyone loves sitting around the campfire, if your group stays up late at night, remember that many other campers are trying to sleep.

7. *Keep your fire under control.* Although you may enjoy a bonfire, the smoke and light can become intrusive and overwhelming to your camp site neighbors. Large fires may also be against park regulations and can become hard to manage.

8. *Don't leave trash at your camp site.* The smell will bring many visitors while you sleep or when you leave your site for a hike. Raccoons or other critters will make noise fighting for the food scraps and will often drag the trash throughout the park. Take your trash to the park-provided garbage bins and recycling containers.

9. *Don't wash your dishes at the water fountain or tap.* When filling up a water container at the water tap, no one wants to wait while others wash dishes, which also leaves a mess and odors that are unpleasant. Wash dishes at your camp site and dump any remaining waste water in the waste vault or park-provided location.

10. *Introduce yourself to your camp site neighbors.* There is no better way to start off your camping vacation then to say "hello" and introduce yourself to your camp site neighbors. Knowing your neighbors helps with camp site security while you are away from your site, and may come in handy if you forgot any items at home like sugar or sun block.

Camping with Kids

Everyone who has children and enjoys camping knows it can be a challenge. If you are an avid camper and are thinking about camping with new additions to your family, you need to be prepared.

Actually, camping with small babies is a lot easier than you think; the majority of babies love to sleep so they don't require as much attention as a toddler.

Toddlers present more of a challenge, as this is the age when they like to explore and touch everything. It's important to keep a close eye on them, as they can wander. The least amount of time spent lounging in one place the better. If you're moving around a lot it prevents them from stopping every couple of seconds to pick up something or wandering off.

However, if you plan on spending most of your time at your camp site it is wise to be prepared. Have toys and games readily available to keep your child occupied, otherwise chances are you won't have much of an opportunity to lounge.

Toddlers may be challenging but can be eased into activities such as camping and hiking. Of course it is wise to prepare them long before your camping vacation. You can start by taking you toddlers on walks to the park and around the block. You almost have to build up their stamina so they get used to walking farther distances. You'll be surprised when you embark on your hiking adventure.

Six to eight years old is a tricky age. It's hard to keep them interested in adult things. It's important to incorporate your child's interests with yours. Include your children in the planning of your trip, as this will help get them excited and want to be apart of it more.

When children are between the ages of nine and twelve, it is probably the best time to embark on your traveling adventures. Before heading to your travel destination find out what the local attractions are outside your camping spot and let your kids loose. Let your kids explore on their own. It'll teach the responsibility and give them a sense of their own camping adventures.

Camping with teens can prove to be a huge challenge, especially if you want them to participate. This means you have to keep them involved in the trip plans at all times. Your best bet is to allow your teenager to bring along a friend. The teen years are a finicky age and it is best to let young adults have some time to themselves.

Tent Camping

Most first-time campers start out with "tent camping." Tent camping is very popular and some love to tent camping so much that they never try any other type of camping. The following tent camping tips are useful when deciding what tent to purchase.

How to Choose a Tent

Tents are extremely useful in all our camping endeavors. It's important to learn how to select the appropriate tent in order to meet your specific needs. Tents provide a place of privacy and provide security once zipped up. Tents also protect us from the weather and bugs, not to mention creepy nightcrawlers.

Backpacking tents fall into two general categories: three-season, which are commonly used for general backpacking, and four-season for mountaineering or winter season camping.

Three-season tents are intended for spring, summer, and fall usage and are the best for ventilation. Three-season fabric is generally a bit lighter than that used for four-season tents. It is very sturdy and will perform well in weather conditions such as rain and wind.

Three-season-plus tents are the new generation of convertible tents. They provide year-round protection and are the most adaptable to any weather condition. Three-season-plus convertible tents contain features such as excellent ventilation through mesh windows, sky and door panels. All openings can be zipped closed for added warmth and protection against wet conditions. A convertible tent usually involves the non-use of one or two poles from the tent's four-season design.

Four-season tents have a sturdy pole configuration and integrate four or mour poles into their designs to help fortify walls and help them stand firm against severe wind or heavy snow loads. They are generally larger in diameter, their material is approximately 10 to 20 percent heavier than that of a three-season model, and the floor of the tent is more durable and resistant to moisture.

Expedition tents offer the same features as a four-season tent plus added living space. They generally contain larger vestibules and at least two doors. They use heavier material and sturdier fabric around the pole sleeves and guy attachments. Expedition tents are specifically designed for mountaineering and ski trips.

Single-wall tents are in the same family as the expedition tent but are more specifically designed to be as small and light as possible and to be able to withstand the most extreme mountain conditions. The single-wall is fast and easy to set up and is designed to be used in cool or dry air conditions in the mountains. If exposed to any other conditions the single-wall requires a large amount of ventilation. Single-wall shelters can also be used on big wall ascents. Some single-walls are specially designed to fit some port ledges.

Bivy sacks can also be used as a form of a shelter but offer very little space and room except for a sleeping bag. Bivys are more commonly used on steep rock faces and are more practical for that purpose than tents.

Tent Tips

Any tent that doesn't require stakes is very handy. Freestanding tents can be moved easily and are good for when you need to shake out debris from inside the tent. Keep in mind extremely lightweight tents are rarely freestanding. Capacity ratings generally tend to be off. Presume it sleeps one less person than what is stated. Try and use a tarp that is waterproof to extend the life of a tent's floor.

Tent Camping Checklist

- ❑ Tent (poles, pegs and rope)
- ❑ Flashlight and batteries
- ❑ Sleeping bags
- ❑ Air mattress or sleeping pads
- ❑ Waterproof matches or lighter
- ❑ Small axe
- ❑ Folding chairs
- ❑ Tarp(s) with rope or cord
- ❑ Knife
- ❑ Lantern
- ❑ Insect repellent
- ❑ Sunscreen

Water Camping

Camping near the water's edge requires special skills. It is important to learn low-impact camping methods, especially when traveling by water, as these ecosystems are extremely fragile.

It is important when you do find a spot to camp that you remove any sign that you spent the night there the next day. This requires the removal of all garbage, food, and gear. Leave it cleaner than it was prior to your arrival.

Choosing Your Camp Site

It is important when paddling to have a map handy at all times to locate various stopping points. Keep in mind locations selected earlier in the day may not be feasible to reach by night, so make sure you have backup points mapped out. Having a map helps you to familiarize yourself with your day's paddling route and to select various break spots.

When selecting your own camp site keep these rules and tips in mind: All camp sites should be located no less than 100 feet away from all water sources to avoid contamination. You should also place your camp away from vegetation.

Setting up Camp

There are a number of important jobs involved in setting up camp for the night. Approach the process as a team effort. After unloading your boats, make sure they're secure for the night by carrying them up and away from the water's edge.

After the boats are safe, establish camp by collecting water, setting up the tent(s), and laying out the camp kitchen. Divide the work up among group members. Try to alternate these duties throughout your trip so people don't get bored doing the same jobs day after day.

Camp Cleanliness/Personal Hygiene

To avoid contaminating fresh water supplies, ensure you wash your dishes, clothes, and yourself far away from all water sources. Always use biodegradable soaps and shampoos.

When nature calls dig a small hole at least five to seven inches deep and at least 250 feet away from all water, camp sites, and trails. After you have finished, cover up the hole completely. Burn the toilet paper or seal it in a bag and dispose of it at a later date.

Winter Camping Tips

Winter camping can be exciting but can also be dangerous if the proper precautions are not taken.

Clothing

It is extremely imperative that you dress appropriately to prevent hypothermia. Always ensure you wear a hat. By covering your head you are preventing heat loss, which contributes to your body's overall blood flow (heat). Balaclavas are also popular to keep other parts of your face from frostbite. They cover your nose, mouth, and neck, and work well in cold, harsh conditions.

It is important to wear layers. Try to stay away from cotton undershirts, as these lock moisture in. Wear a thermal undershirt, which can be found in your local department stores. Look for the ones made of poly, as most contain cotton or cotton blends. Wear a wool sweater overtop your thermal undershirt—this is a great insulator.

It is important to select high-quality gloves. There is nothing worse than putting on a pair of gloves and your hands are cold within minutes. Buy longer gloves as they provide insulation, or choose a style which best suits your needs. You can always layer gloves.

Your legs require layering attention as well. Wear long johns and wool pants overtop and a snow or wind-breaking pant that helps repel water and keep your pants dry.

Your feet require extra attention. Ensure your feet are not only warm but dry. You want a boot that will produce the right amount of warmth, but not too much, as this will cause moisture build-up after a while and will result in freezing overnight. To prevent moisture from entering your boot you may want to consider placing sandwich bags over your socks before placing them in your boot. This helps prevent moisture build-up inside your boot. Make sure your boots are waterproof and fit comfortably, leaving enough room for your bulky socks.

Sleeping Bags

When enduring the winter weather you need to think about your nights and how cold it can get. When selecting a sleeping bag that will be most appropriate for your trip, look for one that is rated for the anticipated temperature. You want a sleeping bag that will insulate and keep you warm from head to toe. Your best bet is to go with a mummy-style bag; make sure it contains a draft tube along the zipper and collar. You can purchase such sleeping bags at camping gear stores. In extreme cold conditions it may be wise to purchase a vapor barrier liner, which will add five to ten degrees of warmth. Don't forget to layer before turning in for the night.

You may want to consider bringing along an inflatable mattress as this will help keep you warmer when you sleep. The higher above the ground, the warmer you'll be.

Food and Water
Many first-time winter campers ponder about what foods to pack. It is important to pack a lot of quick and easy meals with substance. Protein and carbohydrates are key when packing your food supplies; they will help you keep warm. Bring lots of water with you, as it will keep you hydrated and prevent hypothermia.

Pet Camping
Campers enjoy bringing along their pets but it's important to recognize their needs, as they may be different from your own. Remember to create down time for your pet; they enjoy relaxation as much as we do.

Your pet must remain in control at all times and must be obedient. Please check your desired destination's pet rules and regulations prior to departure. The majority of parks require a minimum six-foot leash on your pets at all times unless otherwise posted.

Clean up after your pets. There is nothing worse then stepping in dog-do when enjoying a scenic walk on a trail or path. Carry a plastic bag in your pocket for easy clean-up and be sure to tie and toss in the appropriate garbage disposal unit.

Never leave your pet unattended outdoors. Keep them indoors and out of harm's way and provide a comfortable cool environment when you're away. Don't forget to leave enough food and drinking water. Remember to pack your pet's food dish, as they tend to be finicky about odd food bowls.

Watch your pet around people, especially children. As this probably goes without saying it is important to understand the ramifications of a possible situation. The last thing you want is an attack. To prevent this from happening restrain your pet.

Your pet's sleeping arrangement needs to be laid out prior to departing for your camping adventure. It's best to bring along a pet carrier lined with bedding and a blanket cover.

Vaccinate your pet and carry proof of vaccination with you when you travel. Many parks and campgrounds won't let you past the entrance station without it.

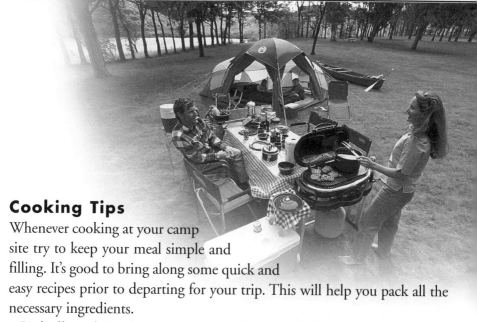

Cooking Tips

Whenever cooking at your camp site try to keep your meal simple and filling. It's good to bring along some quick and easy recipes prior to departing for your trip. This will help you pack all the necessary ingredients.

Pack all meals in plastic containers or bags and label them appropriately. It's also important to bring along a fire grill of some sort, as not all campgrounds provide one. Bring along easy-to-clean or recyclable dishes.

Purchase a quality fuel camp stove that is efficient for cooking and will last you a long time. If you can, cook all food prior to leaving for your camping trip.

Aluminum foil is key for when cooking, so don't forget to pack it!

Fire Pit Cooking

When creating a fire pit, it is important to dig a deep hole approximately two feet deep in a figure eight shape (make the top of the figure eight bigger than the bottom). Light the fire and once coals are hot remove them and place in the smaller hole (bottom of figure eight). Next, place your cooking grill over top and the heat coming off the coals will be sufficient enough to cook food on.

Cooking Checklist

- ❏ Large water jug and water bucket
- ❏ Water filters/purification/ treatment
- ❏ Pots and frying pans with lids
- ❏ Plates and bowls/paper plates and bowls
- ❏ Cooking utensils—spatula, knife, spoon
- ❏ Can/bottle opener
- ❏ Tongs
- ❏ Skewers/grill forks
- ❏ Mugs/paper cups
- ❏ Mixing bowl
- ❏ Measuring cups
- ❏ Thermos
- ❏ Cutlery/plastic cutlery
- ❏ Cutting board
- ❏ Coolers/ice
- ❏ Cooking oil
- ❏ Seasonings/sugar/condiments
- ❏ Stove with fuel/propane
- ❏ Matches/lighter
- ❏ Campfire grill/BBQ grill
- ❏ Fire starters/newspaper
- ❏ Folding table
- ❏ Tablecloth/thumb
- ❏ Tacks/clips
- ❏ Heavy-duty aluminum foil
- ❏ Zip-tight bags
- ❏ Plastic grocery bags
- ❏ Storage containers
- ❏ Napkins
- ❏ Paper towels
- ❏ First aid kit
- ❏ Trash bags
- ❏ Work gloves
- ❏ Dish pan
- ❏ Dish rags/towels
- ❏ Scrub pad/brillo

Camp Stove Cooking

Many campers use fuel stoves as their primary cooking source when campfires aren't efficient enough for a camper's meal. Portable fuel stoves use a liquid petroleum gas cylinder or a propane/butane mix. Fuel stoves can come in a variety of sizes ranging from one to three burners. Multiple burners are more practical for a larger family or gathering.

Camp Stove Awareness

Prior to departing for your camping trip check for any signs of corrosion or any damage to the cylinder valve before filling.

If the cylinder is more than nine or ten years old, your best bet is to buy a new one, but if you want to still use the ten-year-old cylinder it has to be inspected and approved by an authorized testing station.

It is both important and vital for your safety and the safety of others to double check that the connections are sealed before igniting your stove. Never check for leaks around connections with a lit match, as this can cause an explosion.

Never use a stove inside a tent, as carbon monoxide fumes can build up very quickly in small, confined spaces and are very poisonous.

Camping Essentials

Food and Water
Remember to pack an extra two days of food and water in case you wander off course when hiking or backcountry camping. It's best to pack dry perishable goods, as these will last long and no preparation is required.

Water Filter
Sometimes we run out of water and have to resort to the next best thing. Streams, rivers, and lakes provide some of the freshest water sources, but you never know just how fresh it may be. Your best bet is to bring along with you a water filter or sterilizer, as this will purify any water source.

Whistle
A whistle is a great item to have when presented with an emergency situation. The sound can travel far distances. It is important to keep this nearby, as you never know how quickly you may need to use it.

Map
Maps are extremely useful in the backwoods or if you ever wander off trail. A map can help re-trace your tracks if you are ever lost. It is important to have a sense of where you are at all times and to mark your place on the map as you move along. A map can also be useful to help you find water sources when needed.

GPS Unit/Compass
A handheld GPS unit or a compass is a useful tool, and helps campers be

aware of where they are at all times and to stay their destination's course. Make sure you acquire the appropriate navigation skills prior to departing for your trip.

Flashlight

A light is one of the most invaluable items on your list. The moon and campfire can only provide so much light, so be sure to bring along extra batteries or bulbs. Flashlights can also help ward off unwanted wildlife.

Extra Clothing

Don't forget to pack an extra set of clothing. You never know when you'll encounter inclement weather conditions. Whatever you do, do not get your clothes wet, as this can take away your body heat. It is important to recognize that although it may be hot during the day temperatures can drop during the night. So pack appropriately.

First Aid Kit

You never know when you or one of your party will need first aid. It's common for individuals who hike or go backcountry camping to scrape or cut themselves on trees or rocks and you can never anticipate when an injury may occur. It's wise to either purchase a pre-assembled first aid kit or build your own. Be sure to include bandages, antiseptic creams, gauze, adhesive tape, medication, and latex gloves.

Waterproof Matches

Matches aid us in providing warmth, hot food, and light. All are very important and all cannot be attained without a fire source. It's best to pack waterproof matches as you never know what lies ahead and ordinary matches are useless when wet. It is important to be prepared.

Fire Starter

Sometimes it's difficult to get your fire started, so make sure you bring along some homemade fire starter items such as paper toweling, dryer lint, newspaper, wood shavings, and whatever else you may think would make a great fire starter.

Sunglasses

Sunglasses raise a camper's level of enjoyment; there is nothing worse than leaving your shades behind and having to endure the bright sun all day. Sunglasses help you not only to see in sunny conditions but also prevent UV rays from damaging your eyes. Make sure you purchase sunglasses that block out at least 90% of all UV rays.

Sunscreen

Bring sunscreen for the whole family and try to get everybody in the habit of applying it before they go out in the sun. Be sure to purchase a sunscreen with a minimum SPF factor of 15.

Utility Knife

Utility knives are useful for repairs, food preparation, kindling preparation, first aid, and many other useful purposes, and are handy when away from your everyday luxuries at home. Try to buy a multi-use utility knife/tool before your camping adventure.

Bug Repellant

Bugs love the dark sky and love to feast at night, especially those pesky mosquitoes. With the threat of West Nile virus in many regions, they are more than just a nuisance. Make sure you protect yourself and your family with a high-quality, safe insect repellant. Stay away from stagnant water, as this is a breeding ground for many insects. Wear long sleeves at dusk and dawn as extra protection. In places and seasons where bugs are particularly active, you may want to consider hats and hooded jackets with netting to cover the face and head.

Camping Checklists

Hiking Checklist

- ❏ Day Pack
- ❏ Notepad/pen
- ❏ Trail maps/guidebooks
- ❏ Hiking stick/poles
- ❏ Compass
- ❏ Zip-tight plastic bags
- ❏ Water in canteens/water bottles
- ❏ Waterproof matches/fire starters
- ❏ Water treatment system
- ❏ Extra socks
- ❏ Snacks/extra snacks
- ❏ Sweatshirt/jacket
- ❏ Rain gear
- ❏ Whistle
- ❏ Extra clothing
- ❏ Insect repellent
- ❏ Sunglasses
- ❏ Hat
- ❏ Sunscreen/lip balm
- ❏ Money/ID
- ❏ Camera/film
- ❏ Watch
- ❏ Binoculars
- ❏ Toilet paper
- ❏ Bandana
- ❏ Cell phone
- ❏ First aid kit/medications/moleskin
- ❏ Flashlight
- ❏ Pocket knife

Clothing Checklist

- ❏ Bathing suit
- ❏ Hat
- ❏ Rain coat and umbrella
- ❏ Beach towel and blanket
- ❏ Sweatshirt and light jacket

Other Items

- ❏ Binoculars
- ❏ Camera, film, batteries

Canoeing Checklist

- ❏ Floating rope
- ❏ Paddles plus a spare
- ❏ Dry bags
- ❏ Life jacket(s)

- ❏ Wood/kindling
- ❏ Newspaper or fire starter

CAMPING SAFETY TIPS

First Things First

Before heading out with your family and friends please make sure to pack the following items; you never know when they'll come in handy.

1. *First aid kit.* The kit can be useful when you or someone encounters a cut, bee sting, or an allergic reaction. Make sure to pack your kit with all the essentials, from antiseptic creams, bandages, scissors, tweezers, and medicine. It's also valuable to learn basic training in attending to injured individuals.

2. *Emergency supplies.* Make sure you pack a map, GPS unit or compass, flashlight, utility knife, matches, whistle, extra clothing, food, water, bug spray, and anything else that will be helpful in an emergency situation.

3. *Check the weather forecast.* Prior to departure check the weather prediction for the area you plan to visit so you can prepare for inclement conditions. During excursions, watch the sky for changes and when it storms take shelter until it passes. Be sure to stay dry, as wet clothes decrease body heat. It is important to keep gear dry at all times.

4. *Arrive before sundown.* Make sure you plan your trip to arrive at your camp site with enough daylight to set up camp.

5. *Inspect your camp site.* Look for potential hazards such as sharp objects, branches, broken glass, poison ivy, bug infestation, etc.

6. *Build all fires in safe, designated areas.* Make sure the fire source is far away from the tent to prevent unwanted fires. Never leave fires unattended and use only battery-powered lighting when inside a tent.

7. *Keep insects out of your tent.* Limit access and by close the entrance quickly.

8. *Dispose of all trash and waste appropriately.* Remember to recycle where applicable.

9. *Be vigilant when using a propane stove.* Read and follow instructions that come with the stove and propane cylinder.

10. *Be aware of insects.* Learn about the bugs native to the area you will visit and be aware of particular hazards (e.g., Lyme disease from ticks). Stay away from spots where bees, hornets, wasps, etc., might be likely to nest.

Avoid wearing perfumes or colognes when in the wilderness. Do not swat at unwanted bugs, this will only stir them up.

11. *Avoid wildlife encounters.* Make sure your camp site is clean, and do not leave food items, garbage, coolers, scented products such as soap or toothpaste, or any cooking equipment out in the open. Never feed wildlife. To ward off animals, try a flashlight, but never put yourself in danger if you don't have too. Learn about the wild animals local to the area you'll be visiting and find out what to do in case of a surprise encounter.

12. *Practice good hygiene.* Ensure your hands are clean before handling food and after using the washroom.

Wildlife Safety Tips

When camping, wildlife sightings can be both exciting and memorable. Some campers camp specifically for this reason, to view wildlife in their natural habitats. Bird-watching is just one of the popular wildlife attractions in many parks and campgrounds. Follow these simple rules to prevent your wildlife sighting from becoming an encounter:

- Never feed wild animals.
- Always keep a fair amount of distance away. Remember out of sight, out of mind!

If you are an experienced camper, you may remember your first camping trip when the raccoons got into your food or, even worse, a bear showed up. Raccoons and many other animals will be visiting your camp site while you are sleeping or off on a hike, so you need to safeguard your camp site. This can be a very unpleasant situation if you are not prepared, as you may be left without food and have a big mess to clean up. In addition, raccoons will sometimes fight over food they find, making it hard for you and other visitors to sleep.

Many people leave their cooler or food box out at night and learn to regret it later that night or upon returning from a hike or swim. Raccoons are very smart animals and have learned all the tricks of the trade from the many previous campers who visited the park.

Before you go to sleep or leave your camp site make sure you do the following:

1. Clear your picnic table of all food items (snacks, condiments and spices).

2. Clean all dishes in your dishwashing tub and ensure no food traces are left.

3. Bring your garbage bag to the park's enclosed bin; do not leave it around the camp site (the scent alone will bring many visitors).

4. Place your cooler and food container in your vehicle. Tricks like placing heavy items on top of the cooler or food box will not work.

5. Never keep food in your tent. Most tents are made of very thin materials and are no match for a raccoon or bear's teeth and claws.

6. Remember that scented items such as soap and toothpaster can also arouse the curiousity of wild animals, so store these items as you would your food.

7. Always read the park-provided materials or speak with the park management regarding such issues, as some parks will have unique guidelines regarding garbage and local wildlife.

Water and Beach Safety

It is important that everyone learn the importance of water and beach safety. Basic safety tips include learning how to swim. The best thing anyone can do to stay safe in or around water is to learn how to swim. Remember to always swim with a buddy, never alone!

Obey all rules and posted signs and only swim in supervised designated areas. Never consume any alcohol prior to swimming, as it impairs your judgment and coordination and reduces your body's ability to stay warm. Pay attention to weather forecasts and stop swimming immediately upon the first indication of inclement weather.

It is important when on a beach to protect your skin from sunlight. Sunlight contains two types of UV rays: UVA and UVB.

UVA increases the risk of skin cancer, aging, and other skin ailments. UVB causes sunburn and can lead to skin cancer. Limit your sun intake between the hours of 10 am and 4 pm and wear a sunscreen with an SPF (sun protection factor) of 15 and up.

It is important to drink lots of water when in the sun. Even if you are not thirsty it is important to keep your body hydrated to avoid sun stroke. Avoid consuming beverages with alcohol or caffeine in them when in direct sunlight.

Watch for early signs of heat stroke. If you suddenly stop sweating it means you're no longer cooling your body. Watch for a rise in temperature; it can get very high and cause brain damage or death. Other signs include red, hot, and dry skin, changes in breathing, consciousness, and pulse. If any of this occurs call 911 right away and move the individual to a cool place. You can quickly cool a body by wrapping cold, wet sheets around it. Place ice packs under the individual's wrists, ankles, armpits, and on the neck to cool. Watch for breathing problems and make sure their airway isn't blocked. Keep the individual lying down at all times.

Eye Protection: Sunglasses are sunscreen for your eyes and prevent damage that can occur from UV rays. Make sure you wear glasses that absorb at least 90% of the UV sunlight.

Foot Protection: Going barefoot is a common mistake made by many when on the beach or around water. An individual's feet can burn very easily without the appropriate protection. It can also prevent injuries from stepping on sharp objects in the sand.

Children's Water and Camp Site Safety

Maintain constant supervision of children, especially around all pools, streams, lakes, tubs, toilets, and buckets of water. It doesn't matter how shallow the water may be, a child can drown in just a few inches. Never rely on an inflatable or floatable device for flotation, as they can lose air or slip out from underneath a child and can never replace supervision.

Enroll your children in a swimming program to teach them how to swim. These courses encourage safe water practices and help make children aware at a young age.

Enroll in a CPR course. Learning CPR not only provides vital, useful skills and information, it prepares an individual for when an emergency situation presents itself.

It is important for parents to be aware and recognize the importance of camp site safety when camping with children. The safest camp site strategy is to assign a parent or responsible adult to supervise and watch the child intently while the other parent or responsible adult attends to other camp site tasks such as cooking and cleaning, etc.

It's wise to keep children busy while on your camp site. You can do this simply by assigning the kids simple camp chores, such as setting up the lawn chairs or putting their sleeping bag in the tent, etc.

Allow your child to play in the tent but make sure the tent is checked and cleared of all dangers. Be sure to keep an eye on the entrance and listen for your child's voice.

Bring along some of your children's favorite small toys. This will help keep them occupied.

Allow your child to explore. Keep in mind children can easily amuse themselves with just about anything around a camp site such as dirt, twigs, and stones, but it is important to check for any potential dangers before allowing them to do so.

Boating Safety

A lot of campers go camping in efforts to participate in water activities such as boating or fishing. It is imperative that anyone operating or aboard a boat be aware and possess the following knowledge and skills:

Learn to swim. If you encounter any unforeseen circumstances and you have to swim, it is important that you and any other boat guest possess basic swimming skills.

Do not drink alcohol while operating or aboard a boat. Alcohol impairs your judgment, balance, and coordination, and alcohol accounts for half of all drownings involving boating incidents. It is also illegal to have open alcohol aboard small craft in many jurisdictions.

Make sure you have aboard your boat a working and approved coast guard life jacket for every passenger.

Discuss your itinerary with a responsible individual prior to departing on your boating adventure. Provide the individual with details of where you are going, and how long you expect to be gone. This way if something does go wrong, someone onshore will be aware.

Take a boating course. These courses can provide knowledge of vital navigation rules and skills, emergency procedures, and the effects of inclement weather.

Weather watch. It is important to be aware of local weather conditions. Stop boating as soon as you hear or see a storm approaching.

CAMPFIRE TIPS

General Campfire Rules

Please make sure when you and your family are camping, to limit the use of campfires to cooking and providing warmth. Campfires can cause forest fires and the smoke pollutes the environment.

Please be courteous when gathering fuel (wood) for your fire. Be sure to use only fallen wood found on the ground; otherwise, purchase pre-cut wood from your campground or local general store.

It is imperative that garbage not be burned in your campfire. Items such as paper can help accelerate a fire but hazardous toxic garbage producing emissions can harm the environment and may attract unwanted wildlife. Clean out your fire pit prior to departure.

It is vital that you never leave a campfire unattended and always make sure that it has been fully extinguished. To ensure the fire has been completely put out, pour water over the embers and coals to prevent re-igniting.

Building a Campfire

Camping isn't camping without a campfire. It is important you know how to build a proper campfire to prevent any unforeseen danger. Follow these steps and you'll be on your way to enjoying a safe campfire.

Any new fire place/pit must be built away from any trees, wood logs/stumps, and vegetation such as tall grass. A safe building distance should be at least five yards away. This will aid in preventing any spread of a campfire.

Observe the area for any fallen debris or overhanging branches before picking your campfire spot.

Make sure when you are selecting your campfire spot that you place your tent in the opposing winddirection. This will prevent any unwanted smoke from entering your tent.

Make sure your fire pit contains a bed of dirt or sand. This should be approximately two yards wide.

Construct a fire ring around your fire pit with rocks if the camp site's surrounding conditions are dry. Avoid using river rocks from a waterway, as

their moisture content can cause them to explode if exposed to extreme heat.

Have a bucket of water handy just in case a fire starts to get out of control. Additional items that can be helpful are a shovel and an extinguisher.

Any firewood collected should be stacked in a pile away from the fire. Try to keep it a minimum of six yards away from the live fire.

Types of Firewood

One of the first things campers do upon arrival is gather enough firewood to get them through the day. It's helpful to know the different kinds of wood needed for a successful campfire.

There are three types of wood: tinder, kindling, and fuel.

Tinder usually consists of smaller twigs, dry leaves or grass, bark, and household items such as dryer lint, newspaper, or a fire starter candle. All these items light and burn rapidly.

Kindling consists of wood pieces and sticks around an inch or less in size.

Fuel consists of larger wood that keeps the fire going, such as fire logs.

Construct a Campfire

Construct a campfire with the appropriate firewood by starting with a few handfuls of tinder piled in the center.

Ignite the tinder with a match and discard the used match in the fire. Gradually add more tinder. You may need to blow the embers at the base to get the fire going.

When the fire has fully started, gradually add kindling, placing it close together on the fire. Keep adding more kindling until you have a roaring fire going.

Lastly, add the fuel to the fire, one piece at a time, and enjoy!

Building Styles

There are two types of campfires, one for the purpose of cooking and the other for warmth.

A *tepee fire* is excellent for cooking since the heat is distributed to one spot and is the most popular building style among campers. Be sure to place your tinder in the center of the fire pit and surround with kindling and fuel in the form of a teepee.

A *crisscross fire* is commonly used for a long-lasting fire with a lot of coals and is the second most popular building style. This type of fire is great for a thriving campfire. Be sure to place tinder in the center of the fire pit and in a crisscross pattern. Place fuel logs on top, adding more as needed.

Easy Homemade Fire Starters

Fire starters already made prior to your arrival at the camp site will come in handy in damp or wet conditions. Try the following when constructing your homemade fire starter.

1. Pinecones covered with wax.

2. Pack charcoal in paper egg cartons. Put a piece of charcoal in each section of a paper egg carton. Cover with melted wax. Tear apart and use as needed. You can also use sawdust, dryer lint, or pistachio shells instead of the charcoal.

3. Take 100% cotton balls and thoroughly rub Vaseline into them. Keep in a zip-tight plastic bag.

4. Newspaper cut into strips (three to four inches wide). Roll up and tie with string. Cover with melted wax.

5. Bundle 10 to 12 Diamond brand "strike-anywhere" wooden kitchen matches together with waxed dental floss. The heads of the matches should all be pointing in the same direction. Generously soak the bundle of matches (except heads) in melted paraffin wax to waterproof and to provide a long burn time. Dip heads lightly only to waterproof them. Simply strike on flat rock to ignite.

6. Cut a cotton cord into one-inch lengths and soak in melted wax. Let dry and store in an empty film container or a zip-tught plastic bag.

7. "Candy kisses." Use the small, six-inch emergency candles and wrap them up in waxed paper. Tie/twist both ends of the waxed paper to seal in the candle (looks like a salt water taffy candy). Light an end when you are ready to start your fire.

8. Cut waxed milk cartons into strips.

9. Stuff paper towel or toilet paper rolls with paper.

10. Newspaper crumbled into a ball.

11. Dried pine needles.

12. Soak a piece of charcoal in lighter fluid. Coat with wax.

13. Use small condiment or "sample-size" cups. Add a long wick to each cup and fill with melted wax. You can also fill them with sawdust.

14. Stack of small pieces of cardboard covered in wax.

15. Waterproof your matches by dipping them in wax or coating them with clear nail polish.

RECREATIONAL VEHICLES

Purchasing Your RV

Once you've been bitten by the bug to buy an RV, the excitement can tempt you to make quick decisions, which can lead to expensive mistakes, potentially reducing the enjoyment you get from your new purchase. Therefore, its well worth a little extra time spent in researching, planning, and shopping to get the right RV for your needs and budget.

First-time buyers face the

most daunting task in selecting the best RV for their needs, because everything, from brand names to types, terminology, and even the buying process, is new to them. So it's important to understand the various styles of RVs available, and to learn some of the basic "lingo" that you'll encounter as you shop.

Next, talk to other RVers, especially those in the same general age group and income category, as they will likely have similar preferences. Ask them how they use their RVs, what they like about them, and perhaps even more important, what they dislike about them. RVers tend to be a friendly bunch and love to talk about their avocation, so don't be afraid to strike up a conversation.

Early in the planning stage, you'll need to determine how many people your RV will be called upon to house. Consider the next few years, and the changes time will bring. For example, what is your current family size? Are there any children on the way? Are your children getting to that age where they'll be going out on their own? Will you be entertaining grandchildren?

Young families on limited budgets just starting out in the RV lifestyle often choose a lightweight folding tent trailer, which can be towed with the family car. Later, as they have more funds available, and perhaps a larger family, they may move up to a more substantial hard-sided trailer. Larger trailers are, of course, heavier, and require a tow vehicle that's capable of the load. The largest and heaviest trailers are fifth-wheel designs, which are the most stable to tow but require trucks with an open back to accommodate the hitch. People with limited agility may find hitching and unhitching trailers difficult, and may choose a motor home instead.

Lifestyle is another important selection factor. For instance, if you want to tow a boat trailer on your camping trips, you'll have to consider a van conversion, motor home, or truck camper.

For those who camp in cold climates, or want to enjoy winter sports such as skiing, snowmobiling, and so on, it's important to choose an RV that's designed to handle sub-freezing temperatures, with insulated and heated holding tanks and other frost-proofing measures.

Next, estimate how often you can get away, and for how long. Naturally, retirees can usually go away more often and for longer periods than those with a busy employment schedule. Generally, the longer you stay in an RV, the more room and storage space you'll want, and the more it will cost.

Some RVs are more capable of being used for extended periods without campground hook-ups, such as water, electricity, and sewage. These units have larger holding tanks, more liquid petroleum gas, and perhaps an onboard generator or solar panels and larger batteries. If you prefer boon-docking (dry camping) to full-service campgrounds, keep in mind that some of the primitive camping areas have rugged access roads and may not have the room to accommodate larger rigs.

Whether you choose a motor home or a trailer, you'll need to consider motor power. Generally, diesel engines are an optional extra on pickup trucks and some motor homes, or come standard on the pricier coaches. If you intend to cover long distances often with your RV, a diesel may prove more economical due to its lower fuel consumption and longer life. However, occasional users and those who stay near home or operate without electrical hook-ups in below-freezing weather may prefer gasoline power.

Once you have a general idea of what you need and want, it's time to do some comparison shopping. One of the best places to do this is at a large RV show that displays a wide selection of brands, models, and types. Bring along a notebook and take careful notes, because after a while the details of individual models will begin to blur.

After you have narrowed down your shopping to a certain type of RV, you should familiarize yourself with the various floor plans available and decide which you like best. There are also many different available options and accessories, which can customize the coach to your needs.

Typical RV construction uses wooden framing, aluminum siding and roof, lauan plywood interior paneling, and wood-composition cabinets. Upgrades may include a rubberized roof, fiberglass siding, aluminum fram-ing, and solid-wood cabinetry. Of course, interior upgrades are limitless in scope, and include finer fabrics and carpeting, leather upholstery, Corian countertops, and so on.

If possible, try out the various features. Renting an RV that is similar to the one you are interested in buying is an excellent way to tell if this is real-ly the one for you. Sometimes, especially if you have unusual needs and requirements, the best solution is a custom-built RV, although this is best done when you already have some experience.

Take your time and look over the coach from top to bottom, including the roof, inside cabinets, under sinks, and in outside storage compartments. Look for fit and finish, orderly routing of wiring and plumbing, doors that fit well and a lack of rough edges.

Weight ratings and limitations are areas that are overlooked by many RVers. This oversight can lead to costly and dangerous durability and safety problems. Many RVs are advertised with a claimed dry weight, which is far less than what the actual unit will weigh when ready to use, and far lighter than a fully loaded rig.

To help calculate actual wet weights, it's essential to multiply the fresh water, liquid petroleum gas, and fuel capacities in gallons by the weight of the liquids. Water weighs 8.3 pounds per gallon, LP-gas weighs 4.25 pounds per gallon, gasoline weighs 6.3 pounds per gallon, and diesel fuel weighs 7.1 pounds per gallon. Batteries are very heavy and their weight must be included. Water heaters hold about six gallons, which adds about another 50 pounds that nobody usually thinks about. Subtract the calculated wet weight from the gross vehicle weight rating (gvwr) to estimate the payload (cargo) capacity. Motor homes must also include the weight of all passengers.

After you get a general idea of what is available and what the price ranges are, it's time to look at what you can realistically afford. In some cases, you may be able to list your RV as a second home, which offers some savings; consult your tax advisor for specific details.

Besides the cost of the RV, there are other important considerations. Can you park it on your property or do your city's laws allow on-street parking? If not, you may have to pay for off-site parking, which increases your monthly cost. Additionally, take into consideration how much state sales tax will cost initially, and what annual registration will cost. Many dealers offer extended-service contracts and warranties at the time of sale.

Before you sign on the bottom line, talk with several dealerships and shop the deal, but be sure to take into consideration the dealer's reputation, service facilities, and how far the facility is from your home. After all, a good deal is not only about the cheapest price.

Types of RVs

When you start researching your RV purchase, it helps to be aware of the different types available and the industry's terminology. First of all, a recreational vehicle, or RV, is defined as a motorized or towable vehicle that combines transportation and living quarters. RVs do not include mobile homes. The following are specific types of RVs:

Towable Travel Trailer

Ranges from 12 to 35 feet in length, and is towed by means of a bumper or frame hitch attached to a car, truck, or SUV.

Fifth-Wheel Trailer

This unit can be furnished the same as the conventional travel trailer, but is constructed with a raised forward section, allowing for a bi-level floor plan. It ranges from 21 to 40 feet in length. This style is towed by a truck equipped with a fifth-wheel hitch.

Folding Camping Trailer

Also known as a pop-up trailer, this lightweight unit has collapsible canvas sidewalls that fold for towing by a motorized vehicle. It ranges from 15 to 23 feet when opened.

Truck Camper

A truck (or pickup) camper is designed to be loaded on and affixed to the bed or chassis of a truck. It ranges from 5 to 13 feet in length.

Motorized Class A Motorhome

Constructed on a bare, one-piece, specially designed motor-vehicle chassis, the Class A is the largest, most luxurious conventional motor home. It ranges from 21 to 40 feet in length.

Bus Conversion

Also known as a custom coach, a bus conversion is a high-end Class A motorhome, usually characterized by a diesel-pusher chassis. It ranges from 40 to 45 feet in length.

Class C Motorhome

Known also as a mini-motorhome, this unit is built on an automotive manufactured van frame with an attached-cab section. The RV manufacturer completes the body section containing the living area and attaches it to the cab section. It ranges from 20 to 32 feet in length.

Camping Van Conversion

Also called a Class B motorhome, this unit is built on a panel-truck or cargo-van chassis, which the RV manufacturer customizes to include living accommodations. It ranges from 16 to 21 feet in length.

RVing with Children

RVing with children requires additional attention when aboard. Just as parents childproof their homes, they should do the same to their RV.

Here are some easy modifications you should make to childproof your RV:

- Install childproof latches on all the cabinet doors and drawers.
- Attach a dead bolt to the front door of the RV to prevent children from opening it while the RV is in motion.
- Install plastic safety plugs in any unused AC outlets.
- Any items that can be pulled down from high-up places should be moved and put away out of the reach of children.

Try and purchase a RV with bunks for your child's sleeping arrangements. Make sure these bunks are accompanied by safety harnesses to prevent your child from rolling out and off the bunk. Pay attention to the safety guidelines when allowing your child to sleep in a bunk.

To make your trip more enjoyable with your young ones bring along a familiar item that your child is accustomed too. This item could be their security blanket or a stuffed animal—whatever makes your children comfortable while traveling. Don't forget lots of toys and games for the trip too.

Sometimes kids need a break too! Try and stop for regular bathroom breaks and allow your children to stretch their legs. Kids can get quite unruly after a couple of hours of riding in an RV.

Remember, a child loves to be included in everything you do, so try and make them a part of your trip. Include them in your travel planning sessions and come up with activities that will get your kids excited about what lies ahead.

RV Checklist

The advantage of RVing over camping is that the RV is like your second home; it's easier to pack more household amenities. Each person joining the RV excursion should have his or her own checklist of items to bring.

Kids should make a list of items they wish to bring on their trip, such as toys, games, bikes, etc.

Ask your kids what snacks they enjoy and be sure to pack these for your trip.

The rest of the planning will rely on the parents. They should try and get as much help from the kids as possible to pack up the RV. It's important to remember the essentials.

❑ First aid kit (pre-paid or home made)

❑ Medicines (headache medicine, antiseptic, cold medication, etc.)

❑ Toiletries

❑ Linen and pillows

❑ Flashlights and lanterns

❑ Sunscreen

❑ Bug repellant

❑ Matches/lighter

❑ Firewood

❑ Cooking utensils

❑ Silverware

❑ Food and water

❑ And of course anything else you will find useful while on your trip!

Chapter 2: Kids' Camping Adventures

KIDS' GAMES AND ACTIVITIES

ABC Game

Here's a game to while away the time spent travelling in the car or RV. Start with the letter A, then find things that begin with that letter—out in the landscape or on signs or license plates. You can set a quota for each letter—

say, 10 things—and then when the quota is reached, move to the next letter. Or you can make it competitive by making the person who first spots the item that begins with the letter the winner of that round. It gets really tricky when you get to letters like "q" or "x."

Around the Circle

This game is good for grade school–aged children. Have campers join hands and stand in a circle. One camper is "it" and stands outside the circle. "It" walks slowly around the circle, and then taps two campers holding hands on the shoulder and shouts "Around the circle!" "It" takes one of their places. The two tapped campers run in opposite directions around the circle and try to be the first one back to the empty space beside "it." The first camper back joins hands with "it." The other camper becomes "it" and walks around the circle to tap two other campers.

Big Foot

Before you go camping make footprint makers. You can use styrofoam or plywood. Have your child help you to design wild and strange footprints on paper (not too big or your child will fall over). Then trace the image onto styrofoam or plywood and let Mom or Dad cut them out. Attach laces or elastic so they can be tied to the child's feet and you're ready to go! Your child can make strange footprints all around the camp site or if you are camping with more than one child you can play a tracking game—allowing one child to make tracks while others get to track the "beast."

Blind Balloon Volleyball

Teams of four or more people line up in volleyball formation. A blanket is placed over the net so that the teams cannot see one another. The ref throws the ball into play. Each team may hit the balloon as many times as they desire, as long as the balloon doesn't hit the ground.

When they are ready, they send the balloon over to the other team. As soon as one side puts the balloon out of bounds or touches the ground with the balloon the other team scores a point. Add more balloons as the game goes on, up to six.

Bronco Tag

Have the group get into pairs and lock elbows. There is one person that is "it" and another to be chased (you can have two chasee's if there is an odd number of people). The chasee will then run from "it." If tagged they then become "it," but they can reach safety if they then lock elbows with a person. The person on the other end then has to let go and become the chasee.

Bubble Gum Art

Give each participant a piece of bubble gum to chew, a toothpick, and an index card. Allow them 10 minutes to chew the gum, place the gum on an index card, and then design something on the index card using only the toothpick as a tool (no hands). The person with the best and most creative design is the winner. If you have quite a few players you can have several categories of winners, like "most ingenious," "most creative" and of course the "What Is That?" Award.

Bump and Run

Each person draws the name of someone they are to "bump off" at some point later on. The "bumps" will be from a signal agreed upon by the group (a wink, gesture, certain word, etc.) The "bumper" must eliminate their victim at a time when no one else can see it. The doomed victim must then tell the "bumper" who they were to bump off, so that responsibility now goes to the "bumper." Then, later in a public place, the victim "dies," not revealing who their assassin was. And so the carnage goes on, those left alive always looking over their shoulders and looking for their opportunities to strike, until the final player left standing wins.

Camp Parody

Campers take turns imitating a scene while players try to guess what it is. The scene can be camping-oriented or as creative as you would like. Example: playing the guitar or cooking a hotdog over the campfire.

Camping Blanket

One great tradition that many campers participate in and cherish is the camping blanket decorated with colorful badges collected over the years. Most major parks offer badges for sale in their visitor centers or park stores

that have the park logo and often include the prominent wildlife found in that area. When sewn or ironed on a sturdy blanket, these badges bring back fond memories of happy family moments and funny incidents from previous camping trips. Some campers even make it a competition to see who can collect the most badges, and take great pride in having unique or hard-to-find badges from remote areas.

It is recommended that when creating a camping blanket you find one that will last for many years to come. Army blankets are a great option as most are moth-proof, fire resistant, and made to withstand outdoor activities. Army blankets can be bought at army surplus stores and at some sporting goods stores, and are not very expensive. Army blankets usually come in various shades of gray, providing a neutral background for the various badge colors you will be collecting.

Often these badges are produced by associations—sometimes called "Friends of" the park—that help raise funds for the park for use in conservation projects, acquistion of new lands, and other initiatives that will protect these parks so that future generations can experience the same beautiful surroundings that we all currently enjoy. The money from badges and other merchandise offered from these groups will directly support these causes.

If you have the time it is recommended that you sew badges on your blanket, as iron-on badges are more likely to come off down the road, requiring you to sew them on anyway. You may also want to replace your blanket in the future, and badges that are sewn on are much easier to remove and add to a new blanket.

Camping Game Olympics

This is a lot of fun for families or groups with three or more kids. Allow the kids to think up crazy Olympic events (prune spitting, somersaults, pine cone stacking—whatever, as long as it's safe!). Then set the Olympic event into action. This is a great opportunity to put your video camera to use if you have one. Make sure there is an adult present at the finish of each event to prevent arguments—and bring plenty of awards! Everyone should be a winner—and picnic tables work great for the award ceremony.

Capture the Flag

Divide the group into two teams; identify each by a set of arm- or headbands. Set up a jail area (three to four square yards) and a separate hiding spot for each flag. Jails are set up at opposite ends of a five- to twenty-acre area.

The object of the game is to penetrate the other team's area and capture their flag. A flag is "captured" after it has been returned to the captor's jail area.

Prisoners are taken by having their arm or headbands removed by an opponent. Prisoners are taken to the jail of their captor; they wait there quietly until they are released. Prisoners can only be released when a member of their team (with arm or headband intact) runs through the jail in which they are being held captive. After their release, prisoners are given free escort back to a central spot near their end of the area. Here, they are issued new arm/headbands. The game continues until a flag is captured, or time is up.

Encourage teams to plan elaborate strategies of defense and offense. It is fun to play the game with three or four teams, each with its own jail area and hiding spot for flag.

Cat and Mouse

Everyone but two people forms a circle standing far enough away from each other so that a person can safely run past them on either side. They must also be close enough to reach the hand of the person on either side of them.

One of the people outside of the circle is the cat and the other is the mouse. They will begin on opposite sides of the circle.

When the game starts, the cat tries to catch the mouse. If either the cat or the mouse runs through one of the spaces in the circle, the space gets closed. This is done by holding hands.

The game goes on until all the spaces are closed or one or the other gets trapped inside the circle.

Cinderella's Slipper

Two strong brooms are needed for this game. Two teams are formed (three males and three females per team). Each team has a broom. Each of the females removes one shoe. All shoes are put in a large pile at the other end of the playing area. On "Go!," one boy and one girl from each team pair up as follows: The boy grabs the broom handle while the girl steps (crouches) on the broom holding on to the handle. They race to the pile of shoes, with the boy pulling "Cinderella" behind him. The boy must find the girl's shoe (she may not talk!), put it on her foot and pull her back to the starting line, where the next couple is waiting. The game ends when all girls are wearing their own shoes!

Circle Pass

This versatile game can be tailored to your group. Have everyone sit in a circle on the ground or floor and give one person a small ball, bean bag, or other similar item. One person—an adult might be best—stands outside the circle. This person calls out a letter and the other players begin passing the ball around the circle. The person that was initially holding the ball must name a designated number of items before the ball comes back to him or her. For example, players must name five items and the caller calls out "B." The player holding the ball might respond "ball, bat, butterfly, boy, button." When they finish, the caller calls out another letter and the person holding the ball at that time must name five items beginning with the called letter. The caller should pay attention to who is holding the ball and try to ensure that all players have a chance answer.

The number of items players must name can depend on the size of the group and their age. A larger group may call for more items and a smaller group, fewer. As players progress at the game, increase the number of items they must name or ask them to name animals or vegetables or another category of items. This game can be different every time you play.

Cloud Watching

Want to get the kids to unwind? Relax and enjoy the day with a little cloud watching. Just lie back and share what you see—and look for things your children describe!

Crack the Whip

You need at least six people for this game to be effective but the more the better. You all hold hands like you would for Red Rover. Someone is picked to be the leader and someone to be the caboose. The leader just starts running around like crazy and everyone else follows, being sure not to let go of hands. Eventually, after everyone has been running at full speed and making sharp turns, the caboose and/or people next to her or him get sent flying because of the force of everyone running and turning. This is a lot of fun but be prepared to get dirty if you're on the end. Also, the leader and caboose can use two hands to hold on to the one person they are connected to. The caboose tries as hard as she or he can not to let go.

Crocodile Race

Form teams of four to ten players. Each team stands in a straight line. One person is the leader and all the others on the team need to put their hands on the shoulders of the person in front of them. Then the team should crouch down, forming the crocodile. Races can be out to a point and back or whatever adventurous, but safe, idea you can come up with.

"Cross if you . . ."

Have everyone sit in a circle with one person in the center. Players can either sit in chairs, or have place markers (book bags, etc.) behind each of them.

The person in the center names off something he or she has, has done, or can do ("Cross if you have ever jumped out of a plane," ". . . if you own a dog," ". . . have blue eyes," etc.). Those people that can give a positive answer to the question will cross the circle and find an open seat of someone else that answered positively. The caller in the center also looks for an open space in the center.

Since there is one less chair than there are people in the group, and the caller found an opening quickly, there should be one person left in the center. This person then becomes the caller and gets to pick the topic.

Crossed Hands

This game puts a spin on the old saying "The right hand doesn't know what the left hand is doing," and is sure to leave campers laughing. Before you begin, you will need to gather 20 to 50 small objects such as coins, dice, marbles, keys, etc., depending on the size of your group. Divide participants into groups of about 10 and have them sit in lines on the floor or ground facing the other group. Place the objects on the floor by one end of each line. The person sitting by the objects will take one object and pass it to the next person using only their right hands. This person will pass it to next person being sure to use only their right hands. The end person continues to pass items down the line. When the items reach the other end of the line, the last person changes hands and passes the items back up the line using only the left hand. When items return to the starting place, the end person places them in a pile, being sure not to mix them with the items still to be passed. Players continue simultaneously passing items up and down the row until all items have been passed.

Doggy, Doggy, Where's Your Bone?
Players sit in a circle. One player plays the part of the dog, and sits on a chair in the center with eyes closed. An object is under the chair and one of the other players goes over and tries to steal it. Once they get back to their place in the circle, everyone says the rhyme, "Doggy, doggy, where's your bone? Somebody stole it from your home." The "doggy" opens their eyes and has three guesses to find out who the thief is.

Down Knee
Start off with a tennis ball and throw the ball continuously back and forth until somebody drops the ball. When someone drops the ball you say, "Down on one knee," and the person must drop down and continue playing on one knee. If the same person drops it a second time then you say, "Down on two knees." If the same person drops the ball again you say, "Down on one elbow." If it happens again you say, "Down on two elbows." It then goes to chin and then you're out but remember you have to stay in the position you're in to catch the ball and throw the ball.

Everybody's It Tag
Proclaim, "Everybody's it!" in an open space and the participants begin trying to tag others, while avoiding getting tagged. Decide beforehand if simultaneous tags result in both sitting down, or both remaining free. Once tagged, participants sit down, extend their arms, and try to tag those left running around.

Fire on the Mountain
Have the group lie flat on their backs. When you say, "Fire on the mountain," the group has to stand up as fast as possible. The last one up has to then

sit out until the end, or do 10 jumping jacks, push-ups, sit-ups etc. When the group is on their backs they are to lie perfectly still. If you say something other than mountain (Mickey Mouse, Montana, Mazda, etc.) and they flinch or begin to get up, then they must sit out or do the jumping jacks.

First Names

Have everyone count the number of letters in their first name. Now ask them to find someone who has the same number of letters. Those two are now partners. If a person can't find someone, let them use another name they are called by (e.g., a student named Matthew may use the name Matt and then look for someone with four letters instead of seven). If they still can't find someone, they can pair up with a person who has the closest number of letters.

Flashlight Limbo

This is just like the regular limbo dance except using a beam of light as the limbo pole. Use a flashlight and turn off all the lights. Have someone take the flashlight and turn it on and hold it straight. Each player takes turns going under the light beam, and as the game goes on lower the beam. The winner is the person who can go the lowest.

Floating Ball

Using a beach ball or other light inflatable object, the group task is to hit the object, keeping it in the air without letting it touch the ground. Additionally, no one person can touch the object twice in a row.

Set a goal with the group for the number of hits that the group can make following the rules. This fun activity is much harder than it seems.

Follow the Leader

Choose one person to be the leader, and have the other kids follow that person and to do what they do—walk the way they walk, make the same motions, say the same things, etc.

Frisbee Football

Teams should be of equal number; each team has a goalie, as well as offensive and defensive players.

Goal markers are set up at each end of the playing area. The object of the game is to pass the Frisbee past the opponent's goal line to another teammate.

- No player may hold the Frisbee for more than four seconds, without losing possession.
- Three steps may be taken before the Frisbee is passed.
- If offensive and defensive players catch a pass at the same time, defensive players take possession.
- Offensive players are allowed only five seconds at a time in the defensive "red zone" (15 yards from the end zone).

Frog

Everyone sits in a circle. The first person says, "One frog." The next person says, "two eyes," the third person says, "fFour legs," the fourth says, "in the puddle," and the fifth says, "ker-plop!" The next person starts over with "Two frogs" and the game continues as follows: four eyes, eight legs, in the puddle, in the puddle, ker-plop, ker-plop. See how many frogs you can get up to. This may be done to a beat of claps and snaps.

Frozen Tag

In this version of Tag, one person is still "it," but when they touch someone, that person is "frozen" in place. They cannot move and must stand with their feet apart. The only way they can become unfrozen is if a non-"it" player crawls under their legs. Play continues until all the players are frozen. Then the last person to be frozen is "it" for the next game.

Funny Faces

This game doesn't require any props and will delight kids. Have the players stand in a circle. On cue, the players look down at their toes and then up at another player in the circle. If that person is looking at someone else, the player does nothing. If both players are looking at each other, they make funny faces at one another. Play continues. Players must look at only one person and cannot change their gaze midstream.

This activity can also be played as an elimination game. If two players are looking at one another, they are out. Play continues until only two people remain.

Ghost

The first player says a letter. The next person adds a letter, attempting to spell a word. For example, the beginning of a round might sound like this: "E." "N." "G." "A." The one saying the final letter of a word more than three letters long loses. A speller can be "challenged" if the next player doubts that a real word is being spelled. The speller loses if a word cannot be spelled. The loser of each round gets a letter of G-H-O-S-T. The first to lose five times is out of the game.

Good Night, Grannie

Two small tables and two sets of "Grannie"-type clothes (maybe a long dress, night cap, glasses, gloves, shoes—the more and the sillier the better!) plus two candles in holders and two matches are needed for this game. Divide the group into two teams, and have each team stand in a straight line, with several feet between each player. A table is set up at the far end of each line, with the two sets of dress-up items plus candles and matches on top.

On "Go," the first member at the start of each line dresses up as Grannie by putting on the clothes. He picks up the candle and match and runs the few feet to the next player; there he removes the relay clothing to give to the next player. The second person dresses up as Grannie and passes the candle and match to the third person.

The equipment is passed down the line to the final member of the team. When he is dressed as Grannie, he takes the candle back to the table and lights it to signal the end of the relay.

Guess What!

You only need two people to play this game. Both people pick up an object of nature without the other one seeing what it is. They sit back to back and ask yes and no questions about the object. The first to guess what the other one has wins.

Hand and Foot

Have the person or group sit at a table with a piece of paper and a pencil or pen. While they are sitting, have them move their legs from the knee down in a clockwise circular motion. While keeping their feet moving, they have to write a word that you call out (e.g., Australia, eggplant, fireworks).

Heads Down, Thumbs Up

Two or more children, depending on the size of your group, are chosen to stand up and all the others put their heads down with their eyes closed and thumbs sticking up. The two left standing must then creep around and gently touch one person each on the thumb. Everyone is then told to open their eyes and the children who were touched stand up and try to guess which child touched them. If they get it right the children swap places; if not the children have another go.

Human Knot

The group stands in a circle shoulder to shoulder. At this point, you may wish to hand each participant a buddy rope (to help keep heads from bumping each other). Each participant will reach across the circle and hold hands, or the ends of a buddy rope, with two different people (one with the right hand and one with the left). The group task is to get free of the knot without letting go of each other's hands.

Kick the Can

This is played the same as hide and seek, except a tin can is set up in a circle near a designated "jail." The game begins with a player kicking the can. The one person who was chosen to be "it" must retrieve the can and place it back on its starting point. As soon as the can has been kicked, all other players run and hide. If a player is seen hiding by "it" and are called out by name or description they are caught and brought to "jail." If a player can rush in without being caught and kick the can, all who are held as prisoners can run and hide within the space of time it takes for "it" to get the can back in place. One good rule is that a person caught three times becomes "it," or if all are held prisoners, the first one caught becomes "it."

Let's Pretend

This game gives players a chance to use their imaginations. Players stand in an open area. The group leader calls out a scene or an event, such as a picnic in the park, a snowy day, or the Fourth of July. Individually or in groups, players act out what people do on the called day. For example, for a snowy day, campers might pretend to build snowmen, throw snowballs, or curl up inside with a book and a cup of hot chocolate. For the Fourth of July, campers might pretend to watch or take part in a parade, eat watermelon, or view fireworks. After a few minutes, call out another activity and see what campers come up with.

Mother May I?

One person (it could be Mom) stands facing away from a line of kids. She then chooses a child (at random, or in order), and gives an instruction. These follow a pattern, such as, "Brian, you may take "X" giant/regular/baby steps forward/backward." The child responds with "Mother may I?" Mom then states, "Yes" or "No," depending on her whim, and the child complies. If the child forgets to ask, "Mother may I?" he/she goes back to the starting line. First one to touch Mother wins.

Musical Sleeping Bags

This is like musical chairs. Lay the sleeping bags in a circle. There should be one less sleeping bag than the total number of players. Begin the music, and then everyone walks in a circle on top of the bags. When the music stops each person must get into a sleeping bag. Only one person per bag! The person left without a sleeping bag is out.

Nature Scavenger Hunt

Here's a fun way to teach your kids how to pay attention to their surroundings while hiking or camping. Make up a list of items to be found around the campground or during a hike. Be sure to add a few challenging items so it's not too easy. Educate the kids about not disturbing any plants or animals while playing camping games. Remember: "Leave only footprints."

One Up, One Down

One person leaves the group, and the rules are explained. People randomly say "1 up" "1 down" "2 up" "2 down" or some combination of those phrases to describe the position of their arms and legs, and they can move them creatively to change. The person who stepped out needs to try and guess the pattern.

Pencil in the Bottle

This is a hilarious game and can be played either one-by-one or in a team relay. Tie string around a pencil. Kids then tie the string around their waists so that the pencil hangs down behind them about six inches. On "Go" they must then stoop down and insert the pencil into a plastic bottle.

Question Game

Everyone sits in a circle, and each person asks the person to their left (or right—it really doesn't matter) a question. The questions should have interesting answers, not just "yes" or "no" (that makes this game really boring). By the time you get around the circle, everyone should have asked and answered a question. You instruct everyone to remember the question that they asked and the answer they gave to the question they were asked. Those are now the only two phrases they are allowed to say. You then instruct everyone to get up and sit next to someone new in the circle. Then you will go around the circle and people will ask their original questions, and give their original answers, regardless of their question. It is really funny to listen to how it comes out in the end.

Quiet on the Set

All the kids have to be completely silent. Anybody who makes noise is out. Your job is to try to get them to talk. Try asking questions to throw them off guard and to get them to talk.

Radar

Get the group into a circle with one blindfolded person in a chair in the center of the circle to be the "radar." Under the chair place a pair of keys or something that will make a little bit of noise when touched. As the leader, pick out a person from the circle to sneak out and try to get the object. The radar in the center has to then try and figure out where the "sneaker" is coming from by pointing directly at them. If the radar finds the sneaker, then the sneaker will become the radar in the center. If the sneaker is able to get the object, then the radar remains the radar for another round.

Red Light/Green Light

In this game, one person plays the "stop light" and the rest try to touch him/her. At the start, all the children form a line about 15 feet away from the stoplight. The stoplight faces away from the line of kids and says "Green light." At this point the kids are allowed to move towards the stop light. At any point, the stoplight may say "Red light!" and turn around. If any of the kids are caught moving after this has occurred, they are out. Play resumes when the stop light turns back around and says "Green light." The stop light wins if all the kids are out before anyone is able to touch him/her. Otherwise, the first player to touch the stop light wins the game and earns the right to be "stop light" for the next game.

Red Robin

This game works best when played around a tent or building with a fair amount of running space around. Players all begin in front of the tent. Red Robin is the player who is "it." The Red Robin faces the other players and declares, "I'm thinking of a type of (shoe, car, candy bar, etc.)."

The other players then try to guess what the Red Robin is thinking of (for example, a shoe might be Adidas, Puma, Keds, etc.). The Red Robin calls out the name of the player who eventually guesses the correct answer. Then, the Red Robin and the player who guessed correctly take off running around the tent in opposite directions. The first person to make it back to the starting line becomes the Red Robin. (After players get tired, the rules can change to the first person to get back to the starting line is *not* the Red Robin.)

Red Rover

In this game, the kids form two opposing lines and attempt to "break through" the opposing team's line. Two teams are chosen of equal size, and they form two lines, facing each other and holding hands. One side starts by picking a person on the opposing team and saying "Red Rover, Red Rover, send [Jason] right over." Jason then lets go of his teammates and begins a headlong rush for the other line. His goal is to break through the line by overpowering the kids' hold on each other. If Jason breaks through, he chooses one person on the opposing team to join his team, and they both go back and join in Jason's team's line. If Jason fails to break through, Jason becomes part of the other team. Each team alternates calling people over until one team has all the people and is declared the winner. Note that since all the players are on the winning team at the end, there really are no losers in this game.

Rope Push

Split the group into two, and place a line that separates them from each other. Then place a rope across that line with one half on either side. The challenge for the group is to get their side of the rope all the way on the other side and vice versa, at the end of a set period. After a while of trying to throw the rope back and forth, they might figure out that they can simply hand their side to the other while trading with the other team, but that's the challenge, so let them figure it out.

Run Around the Town

A soccer ball and a bat is needed for this game. Divide the group into two teams. Line up the outfield team as you would for a game of baseball. Line up the infield team in a straight line about 15 feet behind "home plate."

The pitcher pitches a soccer ball to the first player, who hits it with the bat. As the ball rolls to the outfield, the batter runs around his team as many times as possible.

Meanwhile, the players in the field line up behind the player who catches the ball. They all stand one behind the other with their legs apart. The player who caught the ball rolls it between his legs and between the legs of his teammates. When the last player in line gets the ball, he yells "Stop!" At his cry, the batter stops running.

The infield scores one point for every three times the batter circled his team. After three batters, teams switch positions. Play continues for as many innings as time permits.

Secret Word

Secretly pick a word. Do not say it out loud. Every time that word is used by yourself or others, do something unusual—scream, put your hands up, clap your hands—until that word is used again. Do this until the other players figure out what your secret word is.

Shoe Scramble

Have all of the participants take off their shoes and place them in a large pile. Then go and mix up the shoes so that no two alike are next to each other. Place the group a distance away. On "Go" they race to the pile, have to place their own shoes on, and back to the starting spot.

Simon Says

One person is chosen to be "Simon." The others stand in a straight line facing Simon. Simon then calls out an action for the children to follow, such as "Touch your toes" or "Jump 10 times on one foot," and so on. When calling out an action, Simon can simply state the action by itself—"Touch your ears"—in which case whoever does it is out and has to sit down. Or Simon can say "Simon says, touch your ears," and then everyone must follow the instruction. The last person left standing can then be "Simon."

Sleeping Bag Game

Make an obstacle course (carefully). Have everyone climb into their sleeping bags and wiggle through it. You can try going under chairs, over stacks of pillows, anything you want. Just be sure you remove all breakable and sharp objects in the play area.

Sock Tag

Everyone takes off a sock and puts it in the back of their pants so that it looks like a tail. The object of the game is to steal other people's socks without having yours taken. If your sock is taken, you must stand on the boundary and you can try to take other people's socks if they come near you (you can only move your upper body). If you steal someone else's sock and you still have your own, you can keep that sock in case your own is taken, then can use your reserve sock as a back up to keep you in the game. The winner is the last person who is left in the middle.

Song Tag

Everyone forms a circle. Someone jumps in the middle and sings a song. Someone else around the surrounding circle can then jump in with a song that is related (for example, Person #1 sings *Old McDonald,* and Person #2 jumps in to sing *Baa Baa Black Sheep* or *The Farmer in the Dell*).
The first person then jumps out and the process continues. Anyone can jump in at any time. The song does not have to be that related, just sung.

Speedy Rabbit

Everyone stands in a circle with the leader in the middle. You first teach the group the various poses of the game. Each pose should use three people. The leader points to one person in the circle, and then that person, and the person on either side of them needs to make the pose that you say. If someone messes up, makes the wrong pose, or moves when they weren't supposed to, then they are out. You can make up your own poses, but here are a few to get started:

- Speedy Rabbit—the two side people face out to make the shape of the ears, and the middle person puts his or her hands in front like paws.
- Screaming Viking—the two side people make rowing motions on the outside, and the middle person bangs their fists on their chest yelling.
- Girl Scout—the two side people put their arms up on a diagonal and lean in to make a house, and the middle person crouches down and says, "Want a cookie?"

Squeeze Murder

This game is played by having everyone sit in a circle. All hold hands, the pre-selected murderer then starts to squeeze the hands of those sitting next to him or her.

For each squeeze, it will travel that many hands away from the murderer. The people next to the murderer squeeze the people next to them minus one time, and this continues until someone is squeezed only once. The person who receives only one squeeze is "dead."

Stand Up, Sit Down

The kids can start out in a standing or sitting position. You ask them questions, such as "Do you have a sister?" or "Are you wearing pink?" If their answer is yes they change to the other position. If no then they stay the same.

Swat the Fly

One person is the swatter. The swatter has either a *very* light stick or large fern or maybe a small foam noodle—something soft so that no one gets hurt. Everyone else is a fly. The flies get in a circle around the swatter. The swatter counts "1, 2, 3, Go!" and the flies run yelling, "Swat the fly!" The first fly swatted becomes the swatter. The swatter continues to swat until he or she gives up or can't catch anyone else.

The Name Game

Here's another in-car game to keep the kids occupied on long trips. Pick a letter of the alphabet and take turns giving a first name beginning with that letter (e.g., C—Carol, Carl, Candy, Carter, etc.) Keep track of how many names each person has come up with. The person who can think of the most names that start with that letter is the winner.

Tongue Twister Race

Print out or write tongue twisters on slips of paper. Pass a tongue twister around and have each person read it aloud. See if you can go around and say it faster each time. To make this more fun, have everyone say it with their tongue stuck under their lower lip, or stuck out.

Trash Scavenger Hunt

Here's a way to have fun and keep your site and park clean at the same time. Make a list of common trash items and assign points for each item collected. For example:

Potato chip bag – 8 points
Candy bar wrapper – 5 points
Bottle cap – 8 points
Plastic six-pack beverage holder –20 points
Plastic shopping bag – 10 points

Print out one of these lists for each player. Set a time limit of maybe half an hour. Then everyone gathers to total up the points for their "collection." Don't put glass and rusty metal objects on the list, as these present a cut hazard. If one of the kid "scavengers" happens to find a dangerous item, they should ask an adult to dispose of it.

Water Balloons

Fill about 10 balloons with water for each team. See if you can throw them to your team members without breaking them.

What Time Is It Mr. Fox?

Mr. Fox starts out at one end of the playing area with his back to the group. The group at the other end then yells out "What time is it Mr. Fox?" Mr. Fox then calls out a time that is on the even hour (one o'clock to twelve o'clock). The group then takes that many steps. When the group gets to where the fox is, but not past him, and asks the time, Mr. Fox can yell "Dinner time!" Mr. Fox then turns and chases the group. Those that Mr. Fox catches are out. The last one left becomes Mr. Fox.

Variation: Allow each player who is tagged to become an honorary fox and help catch the remaining people.

Where Can I Go?

The object of this game is to figure out why the leader responds yes or no to players' requests. Sit in a circle with the leader in the middle. Go around the circle with each player asking the leader if they can go to three different places. If the person pauses and thinks between the places they name then the leader says yes, if they don't the leader says no. The game keeps going until someone figures out the pattern behind the leader's responses. A variation is "What can I bring?" Players name three objects. The secret pattern could be that they all begin with the same letter, or all have double letters in them, are all fruits, etc.

Who Am I?

The group forms a circle. One person is chosen to be the Guesser and they go into the middle of the circle. The Guesser is blindfolded or asked to keep their eyes closed.

Note: Be sure to ask that the Guesser is comfortable playing the game blindfolded. If they are not, let them know its all right and choose another person to be the Guesser.

The game begins with an adult spinning the Guesser around in a circle. The group is asked to spin around in a circle as well, but in the other direction. When the spinning stops, the Guesser points in the direction of one of the people in the circle and says the name of an animal. That person must make the noise that that animal makes. The Guesser will then try to guess who the person is by the sounds they make.

Windows and Doors

Players form a circle holding hands. Then they spread out enough so that everyone's arms are straight out, to form large spaces between them. These are the windows and doors. Then one player starts running, and weaving in and out between the other players. As they do this the players in the circle randomly drop their arms down trying to touch or trap the person weaving in and out. Once the person is caught or touched by the arms of someone, they are out. They then choose which person would be next to weave in and out of the windows and doors.

Wink Elimination

This game is best played in a large group. Sit all of the players in a circle, and have them all put their heads down. Tap one person on the head; this person is the "assassin" and has to eliminate the others by winking at them. If you are winked at, silently count to 10, then safely fall down. If you think you know who the "assassin" is before you get eliminated, you can say you have a suspect. If you are wrong, you are out. If not, you win and the game begins again.

Woody

Here's another travel game. A "woody" is a car, van, etc., that has wooden panel sides. When you see one you yell "Woody" and you get a point. Decide before you start how many points someone has to get to win.

Campfire Songs

Green Grass Grew All Around

There once was a tree
A pretty little tree;
The prettiest tree
You ever did see.
Well the tree was in the hole,
And the hole was in the ground,
Where the green grass grew all around and around
And the green grass grew all around.

And on this tree
There was this limb;
The prettiest limb,
That you ever did see.
Well the limb was on the tree
And the tree was in the hole
And the hole was in the ground
Where the green grass grew all around and around
And the green grass grew all around.

3. Branch . . .

4. Bough . . .

5. Twig . . .

6. Leaf . . .

7. Nest . . .

8. Bird . . .

9. Feather . . .

10. Germ . . .

John Jacob Jingleheimerschmidt

John Jacob Jingleheimerschmidt,
That's my name too!
Whenever I go out,
All the people always shout,
There goes John Jacob Jingleheimerschmidt!
TRA-LA-LA-LA-LA-LA-LA!
(Repeat this chorus about six times, getting softer each time; but sing the
TRA-LA-LA at the same volume every time.)

On Top of Spaghetti

On top of spaghetti
All covered with cheese,
I lost my poor meatball,
When somebody sneezed.
It rolled off the table
And onto the floor,
And then my poor meatball
Rolled out of the door.

It rolled in the garden
And under a bush,
And then my poor meatball
Was nothing but mush.
The mush was as tasty
As tasty could be,
And then the next summer
It grew into a tree.

The tree was all covered,
All covered with moss,
And on it grew meatballs,
And tomato sauce.
So if you eat spaghetti
All covered with cheese,

Hold onto your meatball
Lest somebody sneeze

Big Rocky Candy Mountain

On a summer day
In the month of May
A burly bum came hiking
Down a shady lane
Through the sugar cane
He was looking for his liking
As he roamed along
He sang a song
Of the land of milk and honey
Where a bum can stay
For many a day
And he won't need any money.

Chorus:
Oh the buzzin' of the bees
In the peppermint trees
Near the soda water fountain!
At the lemonade springs
Where the bluebird sings
On the big rock candy mountain!

There's a lake of gin
We can both jump in
And the handouts grow on bushes.
In the new-mown hay
We can sleep all day
And the bars all have free lunches.
Where the mail train stops
And there ain't no cops
And the folks are tender-hearted.
Where you never change your socks

And you never throw rocks
And your hair is never parted.

[chorus]

Oh, a farmer and his son,
They were on the run
To the hay field they were bounding
Said the bum to the son,
"Why don't you come
To that big rock candy mountain?"
So the very next day
They hiked away,
The mileposts they were counting
But they never arrived
At the lemonade tide
On the big rock candy mountain!

[chorus]

A Boy and a Girl in a Little Canoe

A boy and a girl in a little canoe, with the moon shining all around
As they paddled and paddled their little canoe, you couldn't hear another
sound
So, they talked and they talked, 'til the moon grew dim
Then he said, "You gotta kiss me or get out and swim!"
So, whatcha gonna do in a little canoe, with the moon shining all around?

A boy and a girl in a little canoe, with the moon shining all around
As they paddled and paddled their little canoe, you couldn't hear another
sound
So, they talked and they talked, 'til the moon grew dim
Then he said, "You gotta kiss me or get out and swim!"
So, whatcha gonna do in a little canoe, with the

boats floating all . . .

girls swimming all . . .

The Little Bird Song

Way up in the sky, the little birds fly,
While down in the nest, the little birds rest.
With a wing to the left, and a wing to the right,
The little birds sleep all through the night.
Shhhhh! YOU MIGHT WAKE UP THE BIRDS!
The bright sun comes up, the dew falls away,
"Good Morning, Good Morning!" the little birds say.

Three Little Angels

Three little angels, all dressed in white,
Tried to get to Heaven on the end of a kite.
The kite, it got broken, and down they all fell,
Instead of going to Heaven they all went to . . .

Two little angels, all dressed in white,
Tried to get to Heaven on the end of a kite.
The kite, it got broken, and down they all fell,
Instead of going to Heaven they all went to . . .

One little angel, all dressed in white,
Tried to get to Heaven on the end of a kite.
The kite, it got broken, and down they all fell,
Instead of going to Heaven they all went to . . .

Three little devils, all dressed in red,
Tried to get to Heaven on the end of a thread,
The thread, it got broken, and down they all fell,
Instead of going to Heaven they all went to . . .

Two little devils, all dressed in red,
Tried to get to Heaven on the end of a thread,
The thread, it got broken, and down they all fell,
Instead of going to Heaven they all went to . . .

One little devil, all dressed in red,
Tried to get to Heaven on the end of a thread,
The thread, it got broken, and down they all fell,
Instead of going to Heaven they all went to . . .
BED!

Catalina Matalina

Catalina-Matalina-Oop-Scala-Wala-Wala-Hogan-Mogan-Logan was her name.
She had two eyes, upon her head,
One was blue and the other was red.

Catalina-Matalina-Oop-Scala-Wala-Wala-Hogan-Mogan-Logan was her name.
She had two teeth in her mouth,
One went north and the other went south.

Catalina-Matalina-Oop-Scala-Wala-Wala-Hogan-Mogan-Logan was her name.
She had one nose upon her face,
But it wandered and wandered all over the place.

Catalina-Matalina-Oop-Scala-Wala-Wala-Hogan-Mogan-Logan was her name.
She had two hairs on her chin,
One grew out and the other grew in.

Peanut on the Railroad Tracks

A peanut sat on the railroad tracks,
his heart went pitter putter,
along came a choo-choo,
knocked him cuckoo,
now, he's peanut butter . . .

Home On the Range

Oh give me a home where the buffalo roam,
Where the deer and the antelope play,
Where seldom is heard a discouraging word
And the sky is not cloudy or grey.

Chorus:
Home, home on the range!
Where the deer and the antelope play,
Where seldom is heard a discouraging word,
And the sky is not cloudy or grey.

Oh, give me a gale in some Southern vale,
Where the stream of life joyfully flows,
On the banks of the river, where seldom if ever,
Any poisonous herb—i—age grows.

[chorus]

Oh, give me a land where the bright diamond sands
Lie awash in the glittering stream,
Where days glide along in pleasure and song,
And afternoons pass as a dream.

[chorus]

Down By the Bay

Down by the bay where the watermelons grow
Back to my home, I dare not go
For if I do, my mother will say
Did you ever see a goose kissing a moose
Down by the bay?

Down by the bay, where the watermelons grow
Back to my home, I dare not go

For if I do, my mother will say
Did you ever see a fly, wearing a tie
Down by the bay?
. . . Did you ever see a bear, combing his hair . . .
. . . Did you ever see llamas eating their pajamas. . .
. . . Did you ever see an octopus dancing with a platypus . . .
. . . Did you ever have a time when you couldn't make a rhyme. . .

This Old Man

This old man, he played one,
He played knick-knack on my thumb,

Repeated lines:
With a knick-knack paddy-wack
Give the dog a bone,
This old man came rolling home.

This old man, he played two,
He played knick-knack on my shoe,
[repeated lines]

This old man, he played three
He played knick-knack on my knee,
[repeated lines]

Continue using the group's own rhymes such as...
four—on the door
five—on the hive
six—picking up sticks
seven—up to Heaven
eight—on the gate
nine—on a line
ten—with the hen

Oh, Susanna

I came from Alabama
With a banjo on my knee,
I'm goin to Louisiana,
My true love for to see.
It rained all night the day I left,
The weather it was dry,
The sun so hot I froze to death,
Susanna, don't you cry.

Refrain:
Oh, Susanna, oh don't you cry for me,
I've come from Alabama with my banjo on my knee.

I had a dream the other night
When everything was still;
I thought I saw Susanna
A-coming down the hill.
The buckwheat cake was in her mouth,
A tear was in her eye;
Says I, "I'm comin' from the South,
Susanna, don't you cry."

Refrain

I Met a Bear

The other day, I met a bear,
Out in the woods, away out there *[point]*.
He looked at me, I looked at him,
He sized up me, I sized up him.
He says to me, "Why don't you run?
'Cause I can see, you have no gun."
I says to him, "That's a good ideer.
Now legs get going, get me out of here!"
I began to run, away from there,

But right behind me was that bear.
And on the path ahead of me,
I saw a tree, Oh glory be.
The lowest branch was ten feet up,
I'd have to jump and trust to luck.
And so I jumped into the air,
But I missed that branch away up there.
Now don't you fret, and don't you frown,
I caught that branch on the way back down.
That's all there is, there ain't no more,
Unless I met that bear once more.

Yellow Rose of Texas

There's a yellow rose in Texas that I am going to see.
No other soldier knows her, no soldier, only me.
She cried so when I left her, it like to broke my heart.
And if I ever find her, we never more will part.

Chorus:
She's the sweetest rose of color, this soldier ever knew.
Her eyes are bright as diamonds, they sparkle like the dew.
You may talk about your dearest May, and sing of Rosa Lee.
But the Yellow Rose of Texas beats the belles of Tennessee.

Where the Rio Grande is flowin' and the starry skies are bright,
She walks along the river in the quiet summer night.
She thinks, if I remember, when we parted long ago,
I promised to come back again and not leave her so.
[Chorus]

Oh, now I'm going to find her, for my heart is full of woe,
And we'll sing the song together, that we sang so long ago.
We'll play the banjo gaily, and we'll sing the songs of yore,
And the Yellow Rose of Texas shall be mine forever more.
[Chorus]

Take Me Out to the Ballgame

Take me out to the ballgame,
Take me out to the crowd.
Buy me some peanuts and Cracker Jacks,
I don't care if we never get back.
So it's root, root, root for the home team.
If they don't win it's a shame,
For it's 1, 2, 3 strikes you're out
At the old ball game!

Too Ra Loo Ra Loo Ral

Over in Killarney,
Many years ago,
Me mother sang a song to me
In tones so sweet and low.
Just a simple little ditty,
In her good old Irish way,
And I'd give the world if she could sing
That song to me this day.

Chorus:
Too—ra—loo—ra—loo—ral,
Too—ra—loo—ra—li,
Too—ra—loo—ra—loo—ral,
Hush, now don't you cry!
Too—ra—loo—ra—loo—ral,
Too—ra—loo—ra—li,
Too—ra—loo—ra—loo—ral,
That's an Irish lullaby.

Oft, in dreams I wander
To that cot again,
I feel her arms a huggin' me
As when she held me then.
And I hear her voice a hummin'

To me as in days of yore,
When she used to rock me fast asleep
Outside the cabin door.
[Chorus]

He's Got the Whole World

He's got the whole world in his hands; *[Repeat 4x]*
He's got the wind and the rain in his hands; *[Repeat 3x]*
He's got the whole world in his hands.
He's got the sun and the moon . . .
He's got the little bitty baby . . .
He's got you and me brother . . .
He's got everybody here . . .

Bicycle Built for Two

Daisy, Daisy, give me you answer true.
I'm half-crazy all for the love of you.
It won't be a stylish marriage, I can't afford a carriage;
But you'll look sweet upon the seat
of a bicycle built for two.

Henry, Henry, here is your answer true;
I'm not crazy over the likes of you.
If *you* can't afford a carriage, forget about the marriage;
'Cause I won't be jammed, I won't be crammed
on a bicycle built for two.

Clementine

In a cavern, in a canyon, excavating for a mine,
Lived a miner, forty-niner, and his daughter Clementine.

Chorus:
Oh my darling, Oh my darling,

Oh my darling Clementine,
You are lost and gone forever,
dreadful sorry, Clementine.

Light she was, and like a fairy,
and her shoes were number nine,
Herring boxes without topses,
sandals were for Clementine.

Drove she ducklings to the water
every morning just at nine,
Hit her foot against a splinter,
fell into the foaming brine.

Ruby lips above the water,
blowing bubbles soft and fine,
Alas for me! I was no swimmer,
so I lost my Clementine.

In a churchyard near the canyon,
where the myrtle doth entwine,
There grow roses and other posies,
fertilized by Clementine.

Then the miner, forty-niner,
soon began to peak and pine,
Thought he oughter join his daughter,
now he's with his Clementine.

In my dreams she still doth haunt me,
robed in garments soaked in brine,
While in life I used to hug her,
now she's dead I draw the line.

How I missed her, how I missed her,
how I missed my Clementine,

Until I kissed her little sister,
and forgot my Clementine.

Waltzing Matilda

Once a jolly swagman camped beside a billabong,
Under the shade of a coolibah tree,
And he sang as he sat and waited while his billy boiled,
"Who'll come a-waltzing Matilda with me?"

Chorus:
Waltzing Matilda, waltzing Matilda,
Who'll come a-waltzing Matilda with me?
And he sang as he sat and waited while his billy boiled,
Who'll come a-waltzing Matilda with me?

Down came a jumpbuck to drink at the billabong,
Up jumped the swagman and grabbed him with glee,
And he sang as he stowed that jumback in his tuckerbag,
"Who'll come a-waltzing Matilda with me?"
[Chorus]

Up came the squatter, mounted on his thoroughbred
Down came the troopers—one, two, three,
"Where's that jolly jumpbuck you've got in your tuckerbag?
You'll come a-waltzing Matilda with me"
[Chorus]

Up jumped the swagman and sprang into the billabong,
"You'll never take me alive!" said he.
And his ghost may be heard as you pass beside that billabong,
"Who'll come a-waltzing Matilda with me?"
[Chorus]

The Happy Wanderer

I love to go a-wandering
Along the mountain track,
And as a go I love to sing,
My knapsack on my back.

Chorus:
Valderi, Valdera, Valderi,
Valdera-ha-ha-ha-ha-ha,
Valderi, Valdera,
My knapsack on my back.

I love to wander by the stream
That dances in the sun.
So joyously it calls to me:
Come join my happy song.
[Chorus]

I wave my hat to all I meet
And they wave back to me,
And blackbirds call so loud and sweet,
From every greenwood tree.
[Chorus]

High overhead the skylarks wing,
They never rest at home,
But just like me they love to sing,
As o'er the world we roam.
[Chorus]

Oh, may I go a-wandering
Until the day I die.
And may I always laugh and sing,
Beneath God's clear blue sky.
[Chorus]

Head, Shoulders, Knees and Toes

Head and shoulders, knees and toes, knees and toes.
Head and shoulders, knees and toes, knees and toes.
Eyes and ears, and a mouth and a nose.
[Touch the appropriate body part each time it's mentioned. Second time, don'tsay the word "head" aloud, but still touch it. Each verse thereafter, add another body part that you touch but don't say aloud.]

My Bonnie Lies Over the Ocean

My bonnie lies over the ocean,
My bonnie lies over the sea,
My bonnie lies over the ocean,
Oh bring back my bonnie to me.
Bring back, bring back,
Oh bring back my Bonnie to me, to me [x2]
[Action: As you sing each word beginning with the letter B, change from a standing to a sitting position and vice versa. All should be standing at the end of the song. When you have mastered these movements, sing it again, faster.]

If You're Happy and You Know It

If you're happy and you know it
Clap your hands (x2)
If you're happy and you know it
And you really want to show it
If you're happy and you know it
Clap your hands
If you're happy and you know it
- nod your head . . .
- stamp your feet . . .
- shout hooray . . .
- do all four . . .

Boom-A-Chik-A-Boom

I said a boom-a-chik-a-boom! (echo)

I said a boom-a-chik-a-rock!
I said a boom-a-chik-a-boom-
a-chik-a-rock-a-chick-a-boom!
Oh yeah? All right. (repeat)
(Just a little bit louder...)

Sipping Cider through a Straw

The prettiest girl [Echo.], I ever saw, [Echo.]
Was sipping cider through a straw.
[Repeat previous two lines.]
I asked her if, [Echo.] she'd show me how, [Echo.]
To sip that cider through a straw.
Then cheek to cheek, and jaw to jaw,
We sipped that cider through a straw.
Every now and then, the straw would slip,
I'd sip some cider from her lip.
The parson came to her backyard,
A sipping cider from a straw.
And now I have a mother-in-law,
And fourteen kids to call me Pa.
The moral of this little tale,
Is sip your cider from a pail!

Hole in My Bucket

There's a hole in my bucket,
dear Liza, dear Liza,
There's a hole in my bucket,
dear Liza, a hole.
Well fix it, dear Henry,
dear Henry, dear Henry,
Well fix it, dear Henry, well fix it.
With what shall I fix it, . . .
With straw, . . .
The straw is too long, . . .

Well cut it, . . .
With what shall I cut it, . . .
With an axe, . . .
The axe is too dull, . . .
Then sharpen it, . . .
With what shall I sharpen it, . . .
With a stone, ...
The stone is too dry, . . .
Then wet it, . . .
With what shall I wet it, . . .
With water, ...
In what shall I fetch it, . . .
With a bucket, . . .
There's a hole in my bucket, . . .

Found a Peanut

[Tune: Clementine]
Found a peanut, found a peanut,
Found a peanut just now.
Just now I found a peanut
Found a peanut just now.
Continue in the same manner with questions:
- Where d'ya find it . . .
- In the . . .
- What was it doing there . . .
etc until one team gets stuck or repeats.
Then sing "Got you beaten," "repetition" etc.]

The Animal Fair

We went to the animal fair,
the birds and the beasts were there.
By the light of the moon the big baboon
was combing his auburn hair.
The monkey, he got drunk,

and fell on the elephant's trunk.
The elephant sneezed and fell on his knees,
And that was the end of the monk-ey, monk-ey, monk . . .

She'll Be Comin' 'Round The Mountain

She'll be comin' 'round the mountain when she comes. (Whoo, whoo!)
[Repeat]
She'll be comin' 'round the mountain,
blowing steam off like a fountain,
She'll be comin' 'round the mountain when she comes.
She'll be driving six white horses, when she comes,
(Whoa, there!) *[etc.]*
Oh, we'll all go out to meet her when she comes. (Hi babe!)
She'll be wearing silk pajamas when she comes, *[wolf whistle]*
And, we'll wear our bright red woolies when she comes, (Scratch, scratch!)
Oh, we'll kill the old red rooster, (Hack, hack!)
cause he don't crow like he used ter.
Oh, we'll all have chicken and dumplings when she comes, (Yum, yum! /
Yuck, yuck!)
Oh, we'll all have indigestion when she comes, (Burp)

Chapter 3: Top 100 Family Campgrounds

Alexander Springs Recreation Area Ocala National Forest Altoona, Florida

American Legion S F (Hawes) Pleasant Valley, Connecticut

Antelope Island State Park Syracuse, Utah

Bahia Honda State Park Big Pine Key, Florida

Baileys Point Campground Barren River Lake Glasgow, Kentucky

Bear Lake State Park Garden City, Utah

Big Basin Redwoods State Park Boulder Creek, California

Brannan Island State Recreation Area Rio Vista, California

Brevoort Lake Campground Hiawartha National Forest, Michigan

Buckhorn State Park Necedah, Wisconsin

Calhoun Falls State Recreation Area Calhoun Falls, South Carolina

Chief Timothy Park Clarkson, Washington

Chippokes Plantation State Park Surry, Virginia

Chisos Basin Campground Big Bend National Park, Texas

Clarksburg State Park North Western Berkshires Clarksburg, Massachusetts

Colorado River State Park Island Acres, Colorado

Cranberry Lake Campground Cranberry Lake, New York

D.A.R. State Forest Western Berkshires Goshen, Massachusetts

Dead Horse Point State Park Moab, Utah

Defeated Creek Park Cordell Hull Lake Carthage, Tennessee

Del Norte Coast Redwoods State Park Crescent City, California

Dent Acres Campground Ahsahka, Idaho

Devil's Fork State Park Salem, South Carolina

Devil's Lake State Park Baraboo, Wisconsin

Diamond Lake Recreation Area Umpqua National Forest, Oregon

Douthat State Park Millboro, Virginia

Dreher Island Recreation Area Prosperity, South Carolina

Dworshak State Park Orofino, Idaho

Farragut State Park Lewiston, Idaho

Gerald Freeman Campground Sutton Lakes Sutton , West Virginia

Glimmerglass State Park Central Region, New York

Golden Gate Canyon State Park Golden, Colorado

Greenville Recreation Area Wappapello Lake Wappapello, Missouri

Hamilton Branch State Recreation Area Plum Branch, South Carolina

Heckscher State Park Long Island, New York

Hells Gate State Park Lewiston, Idaho

Housatonic Meadows State Park Sharon, Connecticut

Humboldt Redwoods State Park Weott, California

Kendall Recreation Area Wolf Creek Dam Lake Cumberland
   Jamestown, Kentucky

Kings Mountain State Park Blacksburg, South Carolina

Kiptopeke State Park Cape Charles, Virginia

Kohler Andrae State Park Sheboygan, Wisconsin

Lake Erie State Park Allegany Region, New York

Lake Greenwood State Recreation Area Ninety Six, South Carolina

Lake Harris Campground Newcomb, New York

Lake Hartwell State Recreation Area Fair Play, South Carolina

Lake Taghkanic State Park Taconic, New York

Lakeside Beach State Park Genesee, New York

Lepage Park Recreational Area John Day Lock and Dam, Oregon
   (Portland District)

Lewey Lake Adirondack Park Indian Lake, New York

Linville Falls Campground Linville Falls Spruce Pine, North Carolina

Lithia Springs Lake Shelbyville Shelbyville, Illinois

Long Point State Park Thousand Islands, New York

Macedonia State Park Kent, Connecticut

MacKerricher State Park Mendocino, California

Malakoff Diggins State Historic Park Nevada City, California

Manzanita Lake Campground Lassen Volcanic National Park
   Mineral, California

Mashamoquet Brook State Park Pomfret Center, Connecticut

Meacham Lake Paul Smith, New York

Mohawk Trail State Forest Western Berkshires Charlemont, Massachusetts

Moreau Lake State Park Saratoga, New York

Mount. Diablo State Park Clayton, California

Mueller State Park Divide, Colorado

Myrtle Beach State Park Myrtle Beach, South Carolina

Nevada Beach Campground Lake Tahoe Basin Management Unit
  Zephyr Cove, Nevada

Nickerson State Park Cape Cod Brewster, Massachusetts

North Bend Park John H. Kerr Dam and Reservoir Boydton, Virginia

North South Lake Campground Eastern Catskills Haines Falls, New York

Oconee State Park Mountain Rest, South Carolina

Otter River State Forest North Central Baldwinville, Massacusetts

Patrick's Point State Park Trinidad, California

Pearl Hill State Park North Central West Townsend, Massachusetts

Peninsula State Park Fish Creek, Wisconsin

Petersburg Campground J. Strom Thurmond Lake Clarks Hill, Georgia

Pfeiffer Big Sur State Park Big Sur, California

Pocahontas State Park Chesterfield, Virginia

Ponderosa State Park McCall, Idaho

Prairie Flower Campground Saylorville Lake Johnston, Iowa

Priest Lake State Park Coolin, Idaho

Red Fleet State Park Vernal, Utah

Ridgway State Park Ridgway, Colorado

Rio Grande Village Campground Big Bend National Park, Texas

Robert W. Craig Campground Jennings Randolph Lake Elk Garden,
  West Virginia

Roche-A-Cri State Park Friendship, Wisconsin

Rocky Neck State Park Niantic (East Lyme), Connecticut

Salisbury Beach State Reservation North Eastern Salisbury Massachusetts

Salt Point State Park Jenner, California

Salthouse Branch Campground Bassett, Virginia

Santee State Park Santee, South Carolina

Scusset Beach State Reservation Cape Cod Canal Massachusetts

South Sandusky Campground Rend Lake Benton, Illinois

Steamboat Lake State Park Clark, Colorado

Tolland State Forest South Western Berkshires East Otis, Massachusetts

Tub Run Recreation Area Youghiogheny River Lake Confluence, Pennsylvania

Twin Lakes Campground Hartwell Lake Hartwell, South Carolina

Wasatch Mountain State Park Midway, Utah

Watkins Glen State Park Finger Lakes, New York

Wells State Park South Central Sturbridge, Massachusetts

Willard Bay State Park Willard, Utah

Winhall Brook Campground Jamaica, Vermont

Alexander Springs Recreation, Florida

Alexander Springs is a major recreation, scenic, and historical area in the Ocala National Forest. The focal point is a freshwater spring that gushes out approximately 70 million gallons of 72 degree Fahrenheit crystal-clear water daily. It is one of Florida's 27 first-magnitude freshwater springs. The surrounding subtropical vegetation of palms, hardwood swamp and sand pine ridge provide a variety of botanical areas.

The 67-unit campground can accommodate tents and recreation vehicles up to 35 feet. Sixty percent of the sites are reserveable through NRRS and the rest are on a first come, first served basis. The maximum stay is 14 days from April to September and unlimited stays are permitted from October to March. There are no electrical, water, or sewer hook-ups, but hot showers and dump stations are provided. During the summer months there is an interpretive program every weekend at the amphitheatre.

A natural pool offers year-round swimming. Snorkeling is an excellent way to enjoy the abundant fish and swaying underwater vegetation. Scuba diving is permitted in the large spring boil, but valid proof of certification is required. Canoeing is extremely popular all year and offers an alternate opportunity to view Alexander Creek and the adjoining subtropical environment. Canoe rental and canoe rental with back-haul service are offered daily.

American Legion State Forest, Connecticut

The park occupies a total of 3,900 acres located near Barkhamsted, Connecticut. The West Branch of the Farmington River, designated as a Wild and Scenic River by the National Park Service, divides the two forests and is the centerpoint of river-based recreational activities, including camping, trout fishing, canoeing, kayaking, and tubing. Other recreational activities include hiking, mountain biking, hunting, trapping, snowshoeing, snowmobiling and ice climbing.

Seasonal interpretive programs include a nature museum open weekends between Memorial Day and Columbus Day offering displays on forestry, mammals, Native American culture, and local history and culture. Formal presentations on specific topics are held on Saturday evenings between Independence Day and Labor Day. Several guided hikes are offered from May through October.

The Austin F. Hawes Memorial Campground offers 30 wooded camp sites along the river, and facilities include flush toilets, showers, and a dumping station. Other facilities in the forests include day-use recreation areas, picnic shelter and flush toilets.

Antelope Island State Park, Utah

Visitors to Antelope Island State Park drive across the causeway, a narrow two-lane road spanning from mainland to island, leaving the bustle of the Wasatch Front for a refuge of rangelands floating on a desert sea. The island is ideal for families because of its wide variety of recreation opportunities for all ages and abilities.

Antelope Island State Park, the largest island in the Great Salt Lake, is home to a roaming herd of 450 bison. Pronghorn antelope and bighorn sheep also share the rangelands that overlook the desert lake. Opportunities to view wildlife are available on backcountry trails, which are open to horse-back riding, mountain biking, hiking and cross-country skiing. A modern visitor center offers information on the island's unique biology, geology and history. Visitors may also tour the Historic Fielding Garr Ranch House, a working ranch for more than 100 years.

Antelope Island has two campgrounds, Bridger Bay and White Rock Bay Group Area. Bridger Bay has 26 primitive campsites with expansive west-ward views. All campsites have picnic tables, fire pits, grills and vault toi-lets. White Rock Bay has five primitive campsites suitable for large groups. A picnic table, shade cabana, fire pit, and charcoal grill are located at each site, and vault toilets are available.

Bahia Honda State Park, Florida

Any summing up of top campgrounds surely must include Bahia, one of the few subtropical getaways in America and the only place in the Florida Keys featuring 2.5 miles of natural sand, palm-fringed beaches.

With the Atlantic Ocean washing over turquoise shallows to the south and the Gulf of Mexico flowing between mangrove islands to the north, Bahia Honda is 524 acres of enchantment. Temperatures are always mild and each sunny day brings new chances to see rare and endangered wildlife, migrating hawks, shorebirds, or magnificent trees such as the Gumbo Limbo, known affec-tionately as the "tourist tree," for its red, peeling bark.

Just 37 miles from bustling Key West, Bahia Honda draws a year-round mix of families, nature lovers, water enthusiasts, sun-worshipers, and romantics. A single day can include a boat trip and snorkel among tropical fish and coral reefs, a kayak paddle, a picnic under the palms, and a classic Keys sunset from high atop the historic Bahia Honda railroad bridge.

Tent campers can hide away in the shady hardwood hammock near

Sandspur Beach. Buttonwood Campground, on the west end of the island, accommodates almost any size camping rig. Both areas have water and electric on most of the sites and bath houses. Three duplex cabins with a beautiful view of the backcountry islands are also available.

Bear Lake State Park, Utah

Bear Lake State Park is known for its vibrant blue water and white sandy beaches. It also boasts several campgrounds around the southern half of the lake making it an ideal location for families to come and play.

Bear Lake State Park Rendezvous Beach is located on the south shore near Garden City. It extends for 1.25 miles and offers 150 campsites, 3 overnight group-use facilities, modern restrooms, hot showers and utility hookups. A wide, sandy beach provides excellent opportunities for children to play, picnicking, sunbathing, watercraft viewing and swimming. Rendezvous Beach is a popular area for groups and family reunions and the site of an annual Mountain Man Rendezvous. Bear Lake Sails offers small boat rentals at Rendezvous Beach at Bear Lake State Park.

Bear Lake State Park Eastside is located 10 miles north of Laketown and is popular with scuba divers, boaters, and anglers. Six primitive campgrounds provide two, 2-lane concrete boat launch ramps. Drinking water is available at the South Eden campground.

Big Basin Redwoods State Park, California

Big Basin is California's oldest state park, established in 1902. Home to the largest continuous stand of ancient coast redwoods south of San Francisco, the park consists of over 18,000 acres of old-growth and recovering redwood forest, with mixed conifer, oaks, chaparral, and riparian habitats. Elevations in the park vary from sea level to over 2,000 feet. The climate ranges from foggy and damp near the ocean to sunny and warm.

The park has over 80 miles of trails. You will find great information, photos, and videos of some of the most popular trails at the multimedia kiosk in the Sempervirens Room (next to park headquarters).
Some of these trails link Big Basin to Castle Rock State Park and the eastern reaches of the Santa Cruz range. The Skyline to the Sea Trail threads its way through the park along Waddell Creek to the beach and the adjacent Theodore J. Hoover Natural Preserve, a freshwater marsh.

The park has a surprising number of waterfalls, a wide variety of environments (from lush canyon bottoms to sparse chaparral-covered slopes), many animals (deer, raccoons, an occasional bobcat), and lots of bird life—including Steller's jays, egrets, herons, and California woodpeckers.

Brannan Island State Recreation Area, California
Brannan Island State Recreation Area is a maze of waterways through the Sacramento-San Joaquin Delta. This park, northeast of San Francisco Bay, has countless islands and marshes with wildlife habitats and many opportunities for recreation, including boating, windsurfing, and swimming.

One of the outstanding water-oriented recreation areas in the world, the area offers 76 species of birds and great fishing, including striped bass, sturgeon, catfish, bluegill, perch, and bullhead. Frank's Tract, a protected wetland marsh, is home to beaver, muskrat, river otter, and mink.

Brevoort Lake Campground—Hiawatha National Forest, Michigan
The park is located about 20 miles west of St. Ignace, in Michigan's Upper Peninsula. The campground adjoins a 4,233-acre lake that offers a wide variety of recreational opportunities for the camper.

Many of the camp sites have direct access to the water. The sites are large, forested, and have tables and a fire ring. Water and flush toilets are conveniently spaced throughout the campground. A trailer dumping station is near the entrance.
The shoreline on the east side of the peninsula is sandy and suitable for sunbathing and swimming. Species of fish caught in Brevoort Lake include smallmouth bass, crappies, sunfish, perch, northern pike, muskellunge, and walleye. Three trails are available for the hiking enthusiast in search of a short walk or a long trek.

Brevoort Lake is an excellent location for a family planning day trips while camping. Lake Michigan, the Mackinac Bridge, Fort Michilimackinac, and the historic Mackinac Island are easily reached from the campground.

Buckhorn State Park, Wisconsin
Buckhorn State Park is a 4,500-acre peninsula jutting into Castle Rock Flowage and is home to sandhill cranes, deer, turkeys, eagles, Karner blue butterflies, and prairie plants. There are 42 unique backpack camp sites that are accessible only by boat/canoe or hiking trail (equipment carts are available), and 11 rustic drive-in sites, three of which are on the lakeshore.

Breathtaking sunsets are part of the unique lake experience. There are many amenities for disabled visitors, including a furnished accessible cabin and accessible fishing pier, hunting and observation blinds.

Visitors come to the park to fish, hunt, camp, swim, cross-country ski, snowmobile, and hike. Visitors can explore sandblows, savannas, and oak barrens, or the canoe interpretive trail. Spring Fling is the open house event each May with games and activities for families. Naturalist programs are offered on weekends throughout the summer. Two picnic shelters are available for groups to use, and five boat launches providing access to Castle Rock Lake and the Yellow River.

Chief Timothy Park, Washington

Chief Timothy Park, an Army Corps of Engineers facility operated by Northwest Land Management, is located on an island in the Snake River, just a few miles west of Clarkston, via US Highway 12. The campground includes full-hook-up RV sites and restrooms with hot showers. Day-use picnic facilities, a sanitary dump station, a boat launch, and swimming access are also provided.

This park is the eastern gateway into Washington State on the Lewis and Clark Trail and will soon be the site of a unique memorial to the Corps of Discovery by famed architect Maya Lin. This location is also an excellent base from which to explore the Hell's Canyon Recreation Area.

Chippokes Plantation State Park, Virginia

With its recreational activities and opportunities to look at life in a bygone era, Chippokes Plantation, a working farm since 1619, offers something for everyone. Visitors may tour an antebellum mansion, stroll through formal gardens, or view a collection of antique farm and forestry equipment and a sawmill exhibit at the Farm and

Forestry Museum. A campground and three unique overnight cottages allow visitors to spend the night on the historic grounds. The park features an Olympic-size swimming pool, a visitor center with a gift shop, interpretive programs, two children's playgrounds, and opportunities to bike, hike, ride horseback, and picnic.

Chisos Basin Campground, Texas

Nestled high in the Chisos Mountains of the 801,000-acre Big Bend National Park, the campground is situated almost a mile high in the air and surrounded by rugged cliffs. It contains 63 camp sites for those who may wish to escape the sometimes warmer temperatures of the lower elevations.

The drive up the steep and twisting road to the Basin is rewarded with sights that are truly breathtaking. Here, the giant rock formation Casa Grande looms above you, huge dark ravens soar overhead, and The Window beckons you to join it for one of Big Bend's most sought-after sights—a spectacular, multi-hued desert sunset viewed between its two sloping walls.

Several major hiking trails in Big Bend make their start in the Basin. The highest point in the park—7,825-foot Emory Peak—is accessed out of the Basin, as is the awe-inspiring South Rim Trail, which tops out at 7,200 feet and affords an eagle's-eye view of the desert floor 4,000 feet below.

With 450 species of birds either living in or making their way through the park, bird watching possibilities are endless here. Add to that 75 species of mammals, 56 species of reptiles, and 11 species of amphibians, and you have entertainment value for just about everyone in the family. Chisos Basin is a very popular campground for tent campers and RV/travel trailers (less than 24 feet long).

Clarksburg State Park, Massachusetts

Clarksburg State Park is a beautifully maintained, quiet area that is adorned with birch and large red pine trees. The park offers sweeping views of the Berkshire Hills and the Green Mountains. Located just south of the Vermont border, visitors can enjoy canoeing, fishing, hiking and swimming. It is a 5-minute drive to the Museum of Contemporary Art and is 7 miles to the majestic Mt. Greylock.

Colorado River State Park, Colorado

Pack a lunch and enjoy the day along the Colorado River at one of five sections of Colorado River State Park. The park offers great scenery and is a popular area for hiking, biking, picnicking, fishing and swimming near the Colorado National Monument and the Grand Mesa. Fruita, one of the five sections of Colorado River State Park, is a great place to relax or use as a base for a wide variety of area activities. Fruita provides a choice of full hook-ups, electric hook-ups or tent camping.

DAR (Daughters of the American Revolution) State Park, Massachusetts

Located in the foothills of the Berkshire Mountains, the original 1,020 acres were donated by the Daughters of the American Revolution in 1929 as a memorial. Today the forest includes 1,700 acres and has become a lively spot for families in all seasons. Trails are used for hiking and mountain biking. The two man-made lakes offer swimming, fishing, canoeing and non-motorized boating. There are interpretive programs and a pavilion area. There is a group campsite and all individual sites are wooded.

Dead Horse Point State Park, Utah

Dead Horse Point is one of Utah's most spectacular state parks. Towering 2,000 feet above the Colorado River, the park provides a breathtaking panorama of Canyonlands' sculptured pinnacles and buttes. Dead Horse

Point State Park offers picnic areas, restrooms, visitor center, gift shop, sewage disposal, interpretive trail, hiking, and camping.

The Kayenta campground has 21 campsites. Electricity, tent pad, sheltered table and charcoal grills are provided at each site. Modern rest rooms, dishwashing, and sewage disposal are available. All water is trucked in from Moab, so no showers and limited drinking water available.

Defeated Creek Campground, Tennessee

Defeated Creek, located on Cordell Hull Lake, is a beautiful park nestled in the hills of Middle Tennessee. For the nature lover, the park offers a scenic 6.5-mile wilderness hiking trail that provides many breathtaking views of the lake.

The park has two boat ramps that allow easy lake access so that campers can enjoy many hours of fishing and boating. There is also a marina next to the campground that provides boat and jet-ski rentals. Children visiting Defeated Creek will have lots of fun as well. The park contains recreational facilities that the whole family can enjoy, such as two playground areas, volleyball and basketball courts, and a paved bike trail. Visitors can also enjoy a Bluegrass Festival event that takes place annually in the second week of June.

All of the155 sites at Defeated Creek have water and electric hook-ups. In addition, 63 of the sites have sewer hook-ups. There are three bathroom/shower buildings in the campground so that there are always hot showers available for campers.

Del Norte Coast Redwoods State Park, California

The park, near Crescent City and established in 1929, has 6,400 acres with approximately 50 percent old-growth coast redwood and eight miles of wild coastline. The mixed understory includes tanoak, madrone, red alder, big leaf maple, and California bay. Ground cover is dense with a wide range of species. Vegetation is predominately red alder, which will eventually give way to fir and second growth redwood.

The topography is fairly steep with elevations from sea level to 1,277 feet. The predominant mountain range is oriented in a north-south direction with steep cliffs adjacent to the Pacific Ocean, making the bulk of the rocky sea coast generally inaccessible except by Damnation Trail and Footsteps Rock Trail.

Campground facilities include RV dump and fill stations, nine shower/flush toilet buildings, and seven non-flush toilet buildings. Restrooms are cleaned to a sparkling shine every morning in the summer. Hot showers are plentiful and free.

Dent Acres Campground, Idaho

The Campground is surrounded by lush, forested mountains and offers a variety of recreational activities including: boating, fishing, camping and picnicking, along with hunting, hiking and wildlife viewing. The Campground features 50 full hookup sites; restrooms with hot showers, picnic shelters, a playground and boat launch facilities.

Located along the southwestern shore of sparkling, clear Lake Jocassee, this Devil's Fork provides outdoor recreation amid the beauty of the Blue Ridge at the Jocassee Gorges. Lakefront camping, hiking and picnicking are among some of the favorite activities, along with vacationing in the park's contemporary mountain villas.

The park provides access to the cool deep waters of the Jocassee, where anglers try their luck for trout and other species, and boaters drive to remote islands or sites of waterfalls spilling into the lake. Two shaded campgrounds are located near the shores of Lake Jocassee. Restrooms with hot showers are conveniently located in the campgrounds. The main lakeside campground at Devils Fork State Park features 59 paved sites with water and electrical hook-ups. Some of these sites accommodate RVs up to 36 feet. While tent campers may use the sites with water and electrical hookups, a designated walk-in tent camping area includes 25 elevated tent pads with grill pits and centralized water. Boat-in primitive camping is also available and is located on the northern shore of Lake Jocassee at the base of Musterground Mountain

Devil's Fork State Park, South Carolina

Located along the southwestern shore of sparkling, clear Lake Jocassee, Devil's Fork provides outdoor recreation amid the beauty of the Blue Ridge at the Jocassee Gorges. Lakefront camping, hiking, and picnicking are among some of the favorite activities, along with vacationing in the park's contemporary mountain villas.

The park provides access to the cool deep waters of the Jocassee, where anglers try their luck for trout and other species, and boaters drive to remote islands or sites of waterfalls spilling into the lake.

Two shaded campgrounds are located near the shores of Lake Jocassee. Restrooms with hot showers are conveniently located in the campgrounds. The main lakeside campground at Devil's Fork State Park features 59 paved sites with water and electrical hook-ups. Some of these sites accommodate RVs up to 36 feet. While tent campers may use the sites with water and electrical hook-ups, a designated walk-in tent camping area includes 25 elevated tent pads with grill pits and centralized water. Boat-in primitive camping is also available and is located on the northern shore of Lake Jocassee at the base of Musterground Mountain

Devil's Lake State Park, Wisconsin

Geology classes come from far away to view and study the natural wonders here. Rock climbers come from hundreds of miles away. Artists set up painting easels at sunrise. The Nature Conservancy has named the Baraboo Hills, centering on Devil's Lake, as one of "the last great places on earth."

The four campground areas of Devil's Lake provide year-round camping for family tents, pop-ups, motorhomes, and trailers. Wisconsin State Parks continues to support simplicity and a back-to-nature philosophy in its parks. You'll find no lodges or cabins. The 121 camp sites include electric hook-ups. Rangers enforce the quiet hours to support the family-oriented atmosphere. As a courtesy to other campers, generators and air conditioners are prohibited.

Diamond Lake Recreation Area, Oregon

Cradled among the High Cascade volcanic mountains, 3,000-acre Diamond Lake sparkles like a jewel. The lake, at 5,200 feet in elevation, is surrounded by Mt. Thielsen, Mt. Bailey, and former Mt. Mazama, now the rim of Crater Lake.

Camp, bicycle, hike, fish, boat, ride horses, sight-see, or just relax at Diamond Lake. Spring fishing is best and fall camping is spectacular with its glorious golden aspen. This popular area offers diverse recreational activities supported by campgrounds with shower facilities and flush toilets, day-use areas, a recreational vehicle park and a full-service resort with restaurant, store, lodging, boat, and bicycle rentals.

Douthat State Park, Virginia

Douthat State Park straddles Bath and Alleghany counties, nestled in the Allegheny Mountains and features some of Virginia's most outstanding scenery. A 50-acre lake offers swimming, boating, and seasonal trout fishing.

A traditional family park for nearly 70 years, Douthat is listed on the National Register of Historic Places for the role its design played in the development of parks nationwide. Amid some of Virginia's most breathtaking mountain scenery, visitors can enjoy interpretive programs, two miles of stream fishing, a 50-acre lake stocked with trout, a sandy swimming beach with snack bar, boat and bicycle rentals, a gift shop and camp store, cabins, more than 40 miles of hiking and mountain biking trails, a 100-plus-seat amphitheater, playgrounds, picnic areas, tent and trailer camping, and a restaurant overlooking the lake. The park also features two completely furnished lodges that accommodate 15 and 18 guests each.

Dreher Island State Recreation Area, South Carolina

The park is located on Lake Murray, a 50,000-acre reservoir in the Midlands off of I-26. It consists of three islands linked to the mainland by a causeway and two bridges. Its 348 acres and 12 miles of shoreline provide guests with a variety of outdoor water recreation opportunities. The park offers lakeside camping, picnicking, lakeside villas, and a nature trail.

Two lakefront camping areas have scenic views and easy access to the shoreline of Lake Murray. Ninety-seven paved sites may be used by both

RVs and tents, while 15 sites are for tent campers only. Each wooded site has water and electrical hook-ups and a picnic table. Many sites accommodate RVs up to 45 feet, others up to 30 feet. All sites are convenient to hot showers and restrooms.

Park guests can enjoy a relaxing walk along the Billy Dreher Nature Trail, and those a little more adventurous, the 2.1-mile Little Gap Trail.

Dworshak State Park, Idaho

The campground is located among trees and open meadows on the western shore of Dworshak Reservoir. The area is known for its moderate summer nights and mild winter temperatures.

Camping, boating, fishing, swimming, hiking and water-skiing are just some of the many activities that await park visitors. A boat ramp and handling dock provide easy launching most of the year. A fish-cleaning station is nearby to help with the day's catch.

Farragut State Park, Idaho

Located in Lewiston, 30 miles north of Coeur d'Alene on the shores of Idaho's largest lake, is Farragut State Park. Once the world's second-largest naval training station, today the 4,000-acre park provides a multitude of recreation opportunities including picnicking, swimming, boating, hiking, and camping. In addition there is the Farragut Naval Training Center Museum, a model airplane flyers' field, playground, horseshoe pits, and sand volleyball courts. Other facilities include a shooting range, RV dump station, campfire programs, fish cleaning station, and a variety of group camping and day use facilities. In winter there are groomed cross-country ski trails, a sledding hill, and snowshoe trails.

There are 63 developed camp sites, and 121 sites with water and electric. All camp sites have a picnic table, campfire grill, and modern restrooms and showers nearby. Camping is available from the last weekend in March to the last weekend in October, with reservations accepted for dates from the third week in May to mid September. Primitive camping is available during the winter season. Camper cabins are available year round, though services are limited in the winter and access may be limited to snowshoes or cross country skiing.

Gerald R. Freeman Campground, West Virginia

The park is located on the Sutton Lake project, which covers 13,154 acres of magnificent forested mountains and bubbling streams, with the lake itself covering 1500 acres. Forty miles of pristine shoreline provide a variety of habitats waiting to be explored.

Nestled into the headwaters of the lake are158 camp sites, shower houses, launch ramps, playgrounds, and marina. An endless number of activities such as boating, fishing, biking, hiking, swimming, and diving, or maybe just resting and relaxing, entice visitors.

The Elk River Wildlife Management Area offers over 20,000 acres of public land with miles of roads and trails for discovering wildlife. Bird watching enthusiasts can take advantage of the area's Eastern hardwood forest with abundant populations of wood thrush, scarlet tanagers, indigo buntings, Northern Oriole, warblers and other resident and migratory species. Mallards, grebes, mergansers, cormorants, wood ducks, and other waterfowl are common on the lake. The diverse environment around Sutton Lake provides prime nesting habitat during the spring and summer for many species. Fascinating species seen at the lake include bald eagles, common loons, cerulean warblers, and pileated woodpeckers. Turkeys are frequently seen around the lake as well as many other wildlife species.

Glimmerglass State Park, New York

The park is located eight miles outside the pastoral village of Cooperstown and overlooks Otsego Lake, the "Glimmerglass" of James Fenimore Cooper's *Leatherstocking Tales*. The rolling, partially wooded terrain is host to a wide variety of wildlife. An uphill trail through the forest affords a spectacular view of Otsego Lake. Beaver Pond and Woodland trails are picturesque and of interest for the variety of wildflowers, shrubs, ferns, and mosses.

There are 37 camping sites in the main camping area, which is pleasantly situated close to Shadow Brook, as well as near Otsego Lake. A primitive camping site on Beaver Pond is open all year round for the adventurous camper. With its 14 sites around the pond, four of which are for tents only, it will surely appeal to those wishing for a more secluded feeling. The Hyde Hall Mansion, Covered Bridge, and a self-guided Beaver Pond Nature Trail are within park boundaries and open to visitors.

Winter visitors can go tubing, cross-country skiing, ice skating, snowshoeing, snowmobiling, ice fishing, and winter hiking. And for sports buffs, the Baseball Hall of Fame is a short distance from the Park.

Golden Gate Canyon State Park, Colorado

Only 30 miles away from Denver, 12,000 acres of Golden Gate Canyon State Park awaits you with hiking, picnicking, biking and camping among dense forest, rocky peaks and aspen-filled meadows. Golden Gate's five camper cabins and two yurts provide the perfect escape from Denver among the aspen groves and pine-covered hills. The famous Panorama Point looks over 100 miles of the Continental Divide and makes the park ideal for sightseers and photographers. Miles upon miles of mountain trails for hiking, biking and horseback riding and 155 campsites make Golden Gate Canyon accessible to everyone.

Greenville Recreation Area, Missouri

The Greenville Recreation Area is located on the Wappapello Lake Project. This recreation area offers visitors 111 camp sites, bank fishing, boat ramp access, day use area, group shelter, biking, hiking, hunting, and annual special events.

For nearly 150 years, a small town named Greenville was located on the bank of the St. Francis River. As a frontier town, the county seat of Wayne County, and later as a lumber and railroad town, the community that existed here was a commercial and political center for the region. In 1941, the

U.S. Army Corps of Engineers completed a flood control project for the St. Francis River known as the Wappapello Dam. The resulting lake level necessitated the relocation of the town of Greenville to its present site, two miles northeast of its original position. In March 1990 the area was listed as a National Historic Site.

For a journey through the past, visitors to the recreation area can tour the sidewalks of Old Greenville on a self-guided, historic, one-mile walk known as "Memory Lane" and learn about a town and its people who shaped our nation's history.

Hamilton Branch State Recreation Area, South Carolina

The park is located in the western Piedmont of South Carolina on Strom Thurmond Lake, a popular fishing, boating and water recreation destination. The park covers an entire 731-acre peninsula that provides ample shoreline for fishing. It's also the reason why most of the park's camp sites are lakefront and spacious. The rolling terrain supports a variety of wildlife and provides an excellent setting in which to see the natural beauty of the Savannah Valley region.

The campground is spacious, newly renovated, and boasts 140 camp sites with water and electricity along the shores of the lake. Some sites accommodate RVs up to 40 feet, others up to 35 feet. Eight comfort stations, which include restroom facilities with hot showers, are also located throughout the park.

There is good fishing in the lake for bass, bream, crappie, striper, hybrid bass, and catfish. Two boat ramps provide private boat access.

Heckscher State Park, New York

With three beaches, a boat launching ramp, and a swimming pool, Heckscher offers plenty of opportunities for summertime activities. The beaches are located on Great South Bay on Long Island.

There is a pool complex located on the south beach that offers the gentle bay breeze without the salt water. The park includes picnic facilities with grills, a bridle path, a boat launch ramp, playing fields, playground, and 69 camp sites for tents and recreation vehicles. Visitors can also sit back and enjoy a summer concert series with at least one free show by the New York Philharmonic. Bring a picnic basket full of food, a blanket, and get ready for an evening of music under the stars.

Hells Gate State Park, Idaho

Quiet and grassy campsites along the shores of the Snake River await campers to Hells Gate State Park, situated at the lowest elevation in the entire state of Idaho. At just 713 feet above sea level, the low elevation and the long season of warm weather give rise to Lewiston's reputation as "Idaho's Banana Belt."

A large beach and day-use area with a canopy of shade trees and miles of hiking, biking, and horseback trails make the park a popular destination for day visitors as well as campers. A covered shelter and group-use area can accommodate 300 people and may be reserved for family outings, weddings, club meetings or company picnics.

Housatonic Meadows State Park, Connecticut

Housatonic Meadows State Park contains 451 acres located in Sharon, Connecticut, in the picturesque valley of the Housatonic River amid the rugged hills of the Northwestern uplands. The clear, cold river water provides a fine opportunity for fly fishermen to test their skills on the trout and bass. A two-mile stretch of river (including the park shore) is limited to fly fishing. Housatonic Meadows is an ideal setting for a variety of outdoor recreational activities including fishing, hiking, camping, canoeing, and cross-country skiing. The campground contains 97 camp sites located under tall pines on the river banks. Camping facilities include flush toilets, drinking water, gravel parking, and a pay telephone.

Humboldt Redwoods State Park, California

Located along the scenic Avenue of the Giants, Humboldt Redwoods State Park encompasses 52,000 acres, including over 17,000 acres of ancient old-growth coast redwood forest. The park is California's largest redwood state park and includes the Rockefeller Forest, the largest remaining contiguous old-growth coast redwood forest in the world. The trees here are thousands of years old and have never been logged. This forest is as pristine now as it was 100 years ago.

The park offers 100 miles of hiking trails; fishing, canoeing, and swimming in the Eel River; family, group, horse, bicycle, and backpack camps; a visitor center with exhibits and bookstore; scenic drives; and seasonal interpretive programs such as campfires, nature walks, and Junior Ranger programs.

Kendall Recreation Area, Kentucky

Kendall is located 10 miles south of Jamestown, Kentucky, on US Highway 127. Situated below Wolf Creek Dam along the bank of the Cumberland River, the campground, open year round, has 83 camp sites with water and electric hook-ups, two restrooms with hot showers, two dump stations, laundry facilities, public phone, ice, and basketball court. The camp sites range from partially shaded to full shade. The campground accommodates a wide variety of camping, from tents to large RVs.

Whispering Pines Recreational Trail located at the campground is great for biking and hiking and adjoins a wildlife management area with an observation deck. There are two boat-launching ramps that allow boaters and fishermen easy access to Lake Cumberland and the tailwaters of Wolf Creek Dam.

Kings Mountain State Park, South Carolina

The park rests in a picturesque setting adjacent to Kings Mountain National Military Park, a prominent Revolutionary War battle site. This traditional state park, which encompasses 6,883 acres, offers outdoor recreation activities such as hiking trails, picnicking, fishing from rental boats, seasonal canoe rentals, equestrian trails, and more. Guests can also re-live the lifestyles of early pioneers by visiting the Living History Farm. The park was originally built in the 1930s by the Civilian Conservation Corps, and evidence of their stonework and craftsmanship is still present today.

The campground has 116 sites with individual water and

electrical hook-ups. Several sites accommodate RVs up to 40 feet. The campground is convenient to restroom facilities with hot showers. While tent campers may use the main camping area, the park offers10 designated tent sites which include central water. There is also an equestrian campground available.

The park has two trails: The 16-mile Kings Mountain Hiking Trail and a 1.5-mile nature trail. It also has 20 miles of equestrian trails. There is also fishing for bass, bream, crappie, and catfish from a rental fishing boat in the park's 65-acre Lake York.

Kiptopeke State Park, Virginia
Geographically nestled on the Eastern Shore of Virginia, Kiptopeke State Park provides visitors the best location for fishing and bird watching along the Chesapeake Bay. Visitors enjoy 4.5 miles of biking and hiking trails through coastal woodlands with breathtaking views of US Concrete Naval ships, the Bridge-Tunnel and blue waters of the Chesapeake Bay. The park offers a 24-hour lighted fishing pier, and boat ramp for access to some of the finest fishing in Virginia, life-guarded swimming beach, picnic area, and natural area with four boardwalks elevating visitors over the park's extensive dune area.

It is known nationwide for its spectacular viewing opportunities of raptors and songbirds during the fall migration. Kiptopeke offers tent, electric/water, and sewer hook-up sites, yurt and RV rentals, and laundry-bathroom facilities. Whether enjoying magnificent sunsets, participating in interpretive programs, visiting historic fishing communities, or savoring the serenity of the Eastern Shore, people love their Kiptopeke experiences.

Kohler-Andrae State Park, Wisconsin
Kohler-Andrae State Park is located in Sheboygan, home of majestic sand dunes, miles of golden beach, shimmering blue Lake Michigan waters, whispering pines, an abundance of wildlife, and recreational opportunities for everyone. The Wisconsin State Park System honored Kohler-Andrae State Park as the "Property of the Year" in 2003. Located amidst the sand dunes overlooking Lake Michigan, visitors can stop at the Sanderling Nature Center to view interesting displays on the park's wildlife, history, and Great Lakes fishery, as well as flora and fauna. The center has an auditorium for regular programs featuring slide shows, movies, and guest speakers throughout the summer months.

It is an ideal family campground, offering 105 total camp sites, 49 with electrical hook-ups. During the warm weather season showers, flush toilets, and laundry facilities are available in the family campground. The park is open year-round, offering winter camping experiences as well.

There are two self-guided nature trails in the park, the Creeping Juniper and Woodland Dunes Nature Trail, as well as a boardwalk built over the Black River Marsh. The park provides a wonderful family campground with miles of trails, educational programs, and picnic, volleyball, and baseball areas, as well as a breathtaking two-mile stretch of the Lake Michigan shoreline.

Lake Erie State Park, New York

High bluffs overlooking Lake Erie provide a breathtaking view for visitors. The park features a shoreline of over three-quarters of a mile bordering the shallowest part of the Great Lakes. Campers in one of the 97 camp sites or one of the 10 cabins wil enjoy magnificent scenery from each site. Day users can also enjoy the swimming and picnic areas with shelters, playgrounds, and hiking trails that are available to the cross-country skier in the winter months. Bird watchers come during the migrating season where many different varieties of birds set out to make their journey across the lake.

Lake Greenwood State Recreation Area, South Carolina

Beautiful Lake Greenwood lends its name to this park in South Carolina's western Piedmont region. This 914-acre park covers five peninsulas that provide miles of shoreline for lakeside camping, fishing, and picnicking. Boating and hiking are other popular activities at the park.

Built in 1938 by the Civilian Conservation Corps, the park still boasts evidence of CCC craftsmanship in two picnic shelters, the retaining wall at the lake, a boathouse, and a water fountain.

The camping area provides easy access to the shoreline of Lake Greenwood. There are 125 paved sites that may be used by both RVs and tents, while five sites are for tent campers only. Each site has water and electrical hook-ups and a picnic table. Many paved sites accommodate RVs up to 40 feet. All sites are convenient to hot showers and restrooms.

Enjoy fishing in Lake Greenwood for bass, crappie, bream, perch, catfish, and stripers. Three boat ramps provide private boat access to Lake Greenwood, and various water recreational opportunities.

Lake Harris Campground, New York

Lake Harris is fed by the mighty Hudson River in its beginning stages, and is sheltered among large hardwood trees that offer splendid color contrasts throughout the year. While the lake offers many watercraft opportunities, many love visiting the Visitor Interpretive Center or the Santanoni Preserve Historic Site, both close by.

Lake Harris Campground is located on the northern shore of 275-acre Lake Harris. A number of the sites offer a good degree of privacy. Camping equipment from tents to 40-foot RVs can be accommodated. There are 89 camp sites (57 shoreline, 32 off water), hot showers, flush toilets, trailer dump station, recycling center, boat launch, canoe and boat rentals, and a picnic area.

There are trails on the nearby Santanoni Preserve, trails to the summits of Goodnow and Vanderwhacker Mountains, which both have fire towers, and a major trail head to the High Peaks Wilderness Area located at Tahawus. Nature trails can be found at the Visitors Center in Newcomb.

The Adirondack Park Visitors Interpretive Center at Newcomb is only a few miles from the campground. The Adirondack Museum at Blue Mountain Lake is 25 miles to the west.

Lake Hartwell State Recreation Area, South Carolina

The park has 14 miles of shoreline on Lake Hartwell, a popular destination for boaters, anglers, and campers who enjoy easy access to the lake. With its location on the Cherokee Foothills National Scenic Highway 11, and just off I-85, the area also serves as a gateway to South Carolina's mountain country. An impressive collection of fishing equipment is on display in the park's information center. Modern-day anglers, meanwhile, can attest to Lake Hartwell's reputation for top-flight fishing for sought-after species such as striped bass, hybrid bass, largemouth, crappie, bream, and catfish.

The camping area provides easy access to the shoreline of Lake Hartwell. RV and tent campers enjoy 117 paved sites with individual water and electrical hook-ups. Many sites accommodate RVs up to 40 feet. Thirteen walk-in tent sites include tent pads and central water. All sites are convenient to hot showers and restrooms.

There is fishing in Lake Hartwell for largemouth bass, crappie, bream, stripers, hybrid bass, and catfish. Two boat ramps provide private boat access to Lake Hartwell.

Lake Taghkanic State Park, New York

The park, near Taconic and nestled next to Lake Taghkanic in the rolling hills and lush forests of Columbia County, offers a wonderful variety of recreational activities. It has tent and trailer camp sites, cabin and cottage camping facilities, two beaches, picnic grounds, and a boat launch. In addition, the park has hiking, biking, cross-country ski, and snowmobile trails. Ice skating and ice fishing are permitted when conditions are appropriate.

There are three full-service cottages that have all the amenities of home. The units are fully outfitted, with even an enclosed/screened-in back porch facing the water, a picnic table and fire ring for that late-night bonfire.

Lakeside Beach State Park, New York

Lakeside Park, near Genesse, offers a magnificent, panoramic view of Lake Ontario where you can smell the freshness of the surrounding farms and fruit orchards. There are 274 camp sites, each with electric hook-up. The staff at Lakeside has developed wonderful recreation programs that involve the entire family. There is a picnic area, two ball fields, horseshoe pits, and several playgrounds for kids of all ages. Anglers can fish from the shoreline of Lake Ontario. There are four miles of multi-use trails to hike or bike, and in the winter these trails are ideal for cross-country skiing. The views from the trails are spectacular during all the fabulous seasons in New York.

LePage Park Recreational Area, Oregon

LePage Park is located two miles east of the John Day Dam at the mouth of John Day River where it enters the mighty Columbia River. Accessible by Interstate 84, the park offers visitors a scenic 22-site riverside campground with water and electricity, primitive camping, beach facilities, and bank fishing. A boat launch is available year-round that leads to some of the best fishing in the Northwest.

The John Day River is renowned for some of the best smallmouth bass fishing in the nation. As one of the last free-flowing rivers in the Columbia River Basin, the John Day River also offers some of the best wild steelhead fishing in the area, as well as crappie, catfish, walleye, and chinook salmon.

Lepage Park offers visitors a chance to see and stay at one of the many stops along the Lewis and Clark journey to the Pacific Ocean, and is named for Jean-Baptiste LePage, a member of the Corps of Discovery. The Columbia River was also the path for many settlers following the Oregon Trail.

Lewey Lake, New York

This campground is located in the central portion of Adirondack Park, on a 90-acre lake and offers secluded, wooded sites. There are 209 campsites (some designated as accessible for the mobility impaired), picnic area with tables and fireplaces (some designated as accessible for the mobility impaired), flush toilets/hot showers (some designated as accessible for the mobility impaired), trailer dump station, recycling center, sand beach, swimming area, bathhouse, boat launches on Lewey Lake and Indian Lake, hiking trails.

Camping at this area was well established before development of a campground began in 1920. Initial camping was at Indian Lake just north of the present highway bridge, and the campground was known as Lewey Bridge, being named for the hermit and campground resident Louis Seymour. Reachable by only 13 miles of poor roads, the area was initially developed by the Civilian Conservation Corps during the 1930's. Modernization, however, was not attempted until after the development of the present highway.

Linville Falls Campground, North Carolina

The campground has always been one of the most popular along the Blue Ridge Parkway. Seventy sites, for both tents and RVs, are set within a diverse mountain hardwood forest bordered by the lovely Linville River.

The campground and surrounding area feature spectacular views of the scenic falls through Linville Gorge. The waterfall itself is actually a beautiful series of dramatic falls that drop to a deep gorge, accessed by a trail lined with rare virgin stands of white pine and hemlock. The area around the Falls is one of the few places where the Rosebay, Catawba, and Carolina Rhododendron grow side by side. The various trails here include the short walk up Duggers Creek and more strenuous walks along the Linville Gorge. In addition to the campground, there is a visitor center and beautiful picnic area. National Park Service Rangers offer programs and activities for all ages.

Lithia Springs, Illinois

The campgrounds are set next to beautiful Lake Shelbyville, in the heart of Central Illinois, three hours from Chicago and two hours from St Louis, Missouri. The lake offers 11,100 acres of water with countless charming coves for exploring, fishing, swimming, or relaxing.

Lithia Springs Campground, located 2.1 miles north of Route16 and 3.2 miles east of Shelbyville, Illinois, offers 114 camp sites, providing picnic tables, grills, lantern posts, fire rings, electric hook-ups, shade, and a view of the lake. Ten of the sites supply full hook-ups. The campground also offers accessible camp sites, dump station, laundry facilities, showers, flush toilets, a playground, an amphitheater, boat launch facilities, fish cleaning station, and sand beach.

Lithia Springs Marina, a full-service marina, is within walking distance. The marina offers 250 protected slips. Houseboats, fishing boats, and float boats are available to rent. The marina also has sandwich artists available to make sub sandwiches for a meal on the lake.

Long Point State Park, New York

The park is in a remote area, offering a peaceful, relaxing camping experience. Situated on a peninsula facing Chaumont Bay on Lake Ontario, the park is small and almost completely surrounded by water, with great views from anywhere in the park.

Camp sites are fairly open and grass-covered with scattered trees, a playground, and picnic areas. The bay provides a protected harbor for boats, and Lake Ontario offers excellent boating and fishing opportunities. Constant lake breezes keep the park cool and mosquito-free. It is perfect for that family getaway when family time really will mean something special.

Macedonia Brook State Park, Connecticut

The 2,300-acre Macedonia Brook State Park, originated with a 1,552-acre gift from the White Memorial Foundation of Litchfield in 1918. The park's exciting terrain has resulted from the slow wearing down of its hard rock formation base. The Blue Trail crosses Cobble Mountain and several other peaks, offering outstanding views of the Catskills and Taconics. Numerous springs and streams add to the pleasure of hiking.

The land was once the domain of the Scatacook Indians, who derived their name from the nearby confluence of the Housatonic and Ten Mile Rivers. After Kent was settled in 1738, the Indians and settlers shared this area in comparative harmony. During the Revolutionary War, one hundred Scatacook volunteers operated a signal system along the peaks up the river valley. As the original Kent owners moved away or died, many of the woodland parcels west of the Housatonic were sold or left to a commercial and farming settlement called Macedonia.

MacKerricher State Park, California

MacKerricher State Park, on the Mendecino coast of the Pacific Ocean, north of San Francisco, offers a variety of habitats: beach, bluff, headland, dune, forest, and wetland. There are tide pools along the shore, and seals living on the rocks off the park's Mendocino coast. More than 90 species of birds visit or live near Cleone Lake, a formal tidal lagoon. During winter and spring, the nearby headland provides a good lookout for whale watching. The park is popular with hikers, joggers, equestrians, and bicyclists. Fishing is also popular, with trout in two freshwater lakes. The park has a wheelchair-accessible nature trail.

Malakoff Diggins State Historic Park, California

Malakoff Diggins State Historic Park in Nevada City is the site of California's largest "hydraulic" mine. Visitors can see huge cliffs carved by mighty streams of water, the results of the gold mining technique of washing away entire mountains to find the precious metal. Legal battles between mine owners and downstream farmers ended this method. The park also contains a 7,847-foot bedrock tunnel that served as a drain. The visitor center has exhibits on life in the old mining town of North Bloomfield.

Manzanita Lake Campground, California

Manzanita Lake is an extremely scenic site located in Lassen Volcanic National Forest near Mineral, California. Park programs are offered in the amphitheater every Friday and Saturday night during the peak season, and the campground is located near Loomis Museum, which offers information regarding the area, a bookstore, and gift shop, and is the meeting location for other ranger-led activities each day. The campground offers coin-operated hot showers, a camper store, and laundromat.

Manzanita Lake is great for canoeing and kayaking, as no motor boats of any type are allowed. In the summer the lake temperatures are suitable for swimming. There is a great one-mile scenic hike around the lake where you can watch ducks, geese, and squirrels, and look for bear tracks.

The lake is the home of large German Brown and Rainbow trout just waiting for the lucky angler. It is also a very popular fly fishing spot in all seasons except the dead of winter when the lake is frozen.

Mashamoquet State Park, Connecticut

The region was once the domain of the Mohegan Chief Uncas. The name Mashamoquet is Indian for "stream of good fishing" and originally was applied to the entire area. Later, Captain John Sabin built a house here to serve as an outpost and the settlement gradually increased in size. In 1723, parish and township privileges were granted and the town became Pomfret, named after Pontefract in Yorkshire, England.

The present park area is actually a combination of three parks: the original Mashamoquet Brook, Wolf Den and Saptree Run. A large portion of the park was public domain even prior to the State Park and Forest Commission's creation in 1914 due to the foresight of the Daughters of the American Revolution who had purchased the Wolf Den parcel in 1899. The State purchased this section from them in 1924 for the original 1899 price and added it to the first Mashamoquet Brook parcel which had been a gift of former Pomfret resident Sarah Fay. These areas, other purchases, and gifts (notably, in 1957, the 148 acre Hotchkins Wolf Den Farm parcel) have been combined to form the present 900 acre park.

The most famous feature is the Wolf Den into which, on a night in 1742, Israel Putnam crept and shot a wolf that for years had preyed upon local sheep and poultry. Israel Putnam was later to gain fame as a Major General in the Continental Army during the Revolutionary War.

Meacham Lake, New York

Campers at Meacham Lake are provided with a wide-open view of a truly undeveloped area and can hear the Loon calling in early morning and late evening. Aside from a fishermen's paradise, the campground has an activities area complete with Environmental Interpreters, volleyball, horseshoes, kids playground, and bathing beach.

Meacham Lake Campground is located on the north and west shores of the lake, and is the only developed area within the 1,203-acre park. The campground is in a very scenic area, surrounded by the northern mountains and extensive tracts of Wild Forest state land. All types of camping units can be accommodated from small tents to large recreational vehicles. The west side offers primitive and walk-in sites, while the main campground will accommodate both tents and RV's. There are 224 campsites, hot showers, flush toilets, trailer dump station, recycling center, boat launch, picnic area, sand beach with bathhouse, boat and canoe rentals, playground.

Mohawk Trail State Forest, Massachusetts

Mohawk Trail is named for the most easterly tribe of the Iroquois Five Nations who once resided in this area. Many of the original Indian trails are open for hiking. The forest has over eighteen miles of rivers and streams that make for excellent fishing. There is a small swimming area, interpretive programs and it is great location for visiting the many tourist destinations in upper Berkshire County.

Moreau Lake State Park, New York

Moreau Lake State Park sits on a lake that lies amid hardwood forests, pine stands, and rocky ridges near Saratoga, New York. Shady groves of trees shelter picnic grounds and a pavilion overlooking the lake. Wooded campgrounds are quiet and secluded, offering facilities for group campers, as well as tent and trailer sites.

Located on the beach road is Lake Shore Cottage, a full-service accommodation that provides everything from a refrigerator, stove, dishes, and utensils to a screened porch, bathroom with shower, bedding, pillows, and a cozy fireplace.

Sandy beach, nature, hiking and cross-country ski trails, opportunities for boating, fishing, and ice fishing, and proximity to the Saratoga Springs and Lake George areas offer the entire family a memorable vacation.

Mount Diablo State Park, California

Many visitors to Mount Diablo head straight for the summit to enjoy the famous view. Summer days are sometimes hazy, and the best viewing is often on the day after a winter storm when you can look to the west, beyond the Golden Gate Bridge, to the Farallon Islands; southeast to the James Lick Observatory on Mount Hamilton at 4,213 feet elevation; south to Mount Loma Prieta in the Santa Cruz Mountains at 3,791 feet elevation; north to Mount Saint Helena in the Coast Range at 4,344 feet elevation; and still farther north to Mount Lassen in the Cascades at 10,466 feet. North and east of Mount Diablo the San Joaquin and Sacramento Rivers meet to form the twisting waterways of the Delta. To the east beyond Califomia's great central valley, the crest of the Sierra Nevada seems to float in space.

Mueller State Park, Colorado

Mueller State Park anchors the west side of Pikes Peak and extends over 5,000 acres across some of the most gorgeous land in the Rockies. Park visitors can camp in forested areas with flush restrooms and a camper services building nearby. It has 132 camp sites, including 22 walk-in tent sites and RV sites. The campground can accommodate motor homes, trailers, and tents. All camp sites, except the walk-in tent sites, have electric hook-ups.

Myrtle Beach State Park, South Carolina

Located in the heart of the Grand Strand, Myrtle Beach State Park is one of

the most popular public beaches along the South Carolina coast. This 312-acre oceanfront park plays a major role in preserving and maintaining a portion of the natural heritage of South Carolina's coastline. This traditional state park was built by the Civilian Conservation Corps in the 1930s and has the distinction of being the first state park open to the public in South Carolina.

The park includes a campground, cabins, nearly a mile of beach, picnic areas, a fishing pier, and a nature center. In addition, a nature trail provides a rare opportunity to see one of the last stands of maritime forest on the northern coast of South Carolina. Because of this distinction, the forest has been declared a Heritage Trust Site.

The campground consists of 302 sites and provides individual water and electrical hook-ups. Many sites accommodate RVs up to 40 feet, others up to 30 feet. There are also plenty of sites to accommodate smaller units, including tents. All sites are convenient to hot showers, restrooms, and laundromat facilities. The campground is located approximately 300 yards from the beach. The park store (Trading Post) is located in the campground and has limited grocery items, firewood, snacks, and souvenirs.

Nevada Beach Campground, Nevada

Nevada Beach Campground is on the southeast shore of Zephyr Cove on beautiful Lake Tahoe. It offers stunning beauty with sites right on the beach. There are 60 camp sites with flush toilets, drinking water, picnic tables, and fire rings. There are resident staff on site and firewood is available. Gas, groceries, laundromats, and the gambling attractions of Stateline, Nevada, are just a short drive away. Camping at Nevada Beach offers a wonderful vista of Lake Tahoe with Mount Tallac in the distance.

Nickerson State Park, Massachussets

Located on scenic Cape Cod, Nickerson State Park offers 1,955 acres of densely grown pine and oak forest. The park has four ponds used for swimming, boating, canoeing and fishing. There are paved trails for bicycling, interpretive programs and a nature center. Once inside the campground you tend to forget that you are within minutes of the Atlantic Ocean. In

addition, the park manages the Cape Cod Rail Trail, a 23 mile paved trail for bicycling, horseback riding and walking. This park is also within a short drive of the Cape Cod National Sea Shore.

North Bend Park, Virginia

Located in the rolling foothills of the Virginia/North Carolina piedmont, the park is conveniently located between the towns of South Hill and Clarksville, Virginia. Approximately half of the park's 249 camp sites have electricity and water, while all are spacious, shady, and easily accessible. Two group camping areas, five swim beaches, several picnic shelters, two boat ramps, a bike trail, hot showers, and a nearby universally accessible floating fishing pier provide users with all the desired amenities.

The park overlooks John H. Kerr Reservoir, created in 1952 from the historic Roanoke River, where the Occoneechee Indians once ruled. Nearby, the Visitor Assistance Center is open year-round, while the Environmental Education Center is available during the summer months. There, Rangers provide children's activities and family programs in addition to those offered at the 300-seat amphitheater at North Bend. A hiking trail is located nearby along the river below the dam.

North-South Lake, New York

North-South Lake is the biggest and most popular state campground in the Catskill Forest Preserve, offering extraordinary scenic beauty and historical sites. The area around the lake has long provided visitors with exceptional views of the surrounding countryside. It is said that on a clear day, five states can be viewed from the escarpment.

The campground offers access to numerous hiking trails. The short hike to the site of the Catskill Mountain House provides the reward of incredible vistas. Longer and more strenuous hikes can bring you to such spots as Artist's Rock, Sunset Rock, Newman's Ledge, Boulder Rock, and the Kaaterskill Hotel and Laurel House sites.

The campground includes 219 tent and trailer sites, two lakes, two beaches, two picnic pavilion rentals, two picnic areas with tables and fireplaces or charcoal grills, flush toilets, hot showers, boat launch (no motorized vessels), rowboat, canoe, kayak and paddle boat rentals, fishing, playing field, trailer dump station, and recycling center.

Oconee State Park, South Carolina

This popular upcountry state park rests on a high plateau among tall pines and hardwoods in the foothills of the Blue Ridge near the Cherokee Foothills National Scenic Highway. Among the park's 1,165 acres are two mountain lakes and a variety of recreational facilities for visitors to enjoy, including campgrounds, cabins, picnic areas, and hiking trails. The park also serves as the western terminus for the 85-mile Foothills Trail, which crosses the state's crown and ends at Jones Gap State Park. Developed in 1935 by the Civilian Conservation Corps, Oconee State Park still features the craftsmanship of the CCC in preserved buildings and stonework.

The main campground, located near one of the park lakes, offers 140 camp sites with individual water and electrical hook-ups and picnic table. These gravel sites accommodate RVs up to 32 feet. The main campground also has laundry facilities. Each campground is convenient to restrooms with hot showers.

Oconee has seven nature/hiking trails originating in the park, and is also an access point and the western terminus to the 85-mile Foothills Trail. Fishing boats, canoes, paddle boats, and kayaks are available to rent. Enjoy fishing in the park's 20-acre and 12-acre lakes for bass, bream, catfish, and trout when stocked in the winter months.

Otter River State Forest, Massachusetts

The first campground in the Massachusetts State Park system, Otter River has retained its original charm while constantly updating its appeal and services. Campsites surround the tranquil 2-acre Beaman Pond. Visitors can swim, fish, hike, mountain bike and participate in interpretive programs. There is a ball field, 3 group campsites, and yurt camping available.

Patrick's Point State Park, California

Located 25 miles north of Eureka, California, Patrick's Point is a 640-acre park in the heart of California's coast redwood country. The park's dense forests of spruce, hemlock, pine, fir, and red alder stretch over an ocean headland with lovely wildflower-festooned meadows. A dramatic shoreline ranging from broad sandy beaches to sheer cliffs that rise high above the Pacific Ocean offers great opportunities to explore tide pools, search for agates and driftwood, and to watch whales, sea lions, and brilliant sunsets.

The park offers several miles of hiking trails, a reconstructed Yurok Indian

Village, a native plant garden, a bookstore, three family campgrounds, a group camp, a camp for hikers and bicyclist, and several picnic areas.

Pearl Hill State Park, Massachusetts

The park offers some of the largest and most private campsites in the state, all underneath a canopy of stately pines. It is breathtaking in June when the mountain laurel is in bloom and once the weather warms up there is swimming in a 5-acre man made pond created each year by damming the Pearl Hill Brook. The park offers a ball field, interpretive programs, fishing, hiking, and mountain biking. Visitors can bike the nearby 10-mile Nashua River Rail Trail and visit Mt. Watatic for great family hiking.

Peninsula State Park, Wisconsin

Wisconsin's most popular camping destination. Two features dominate its diverse and dramatic landscape—rock and water. Dolostone bluffs surge 150 feet upwards, offering spectacular views. Eight miles of shoreline cradle the rocky promontories. Tje shore is protected, part of a 3,776-acre state park established by far-sighted citizens in 1909.

Peninsula offers 472 family camp sites, nearly 40 miles of hiking and biking trails, 15 miles of cross-country ski trails, 18 miles of snowmobile trails, and a natural sand swimming beach. Eagle Bluff Lighthouse (1868), a 75-foot look-out tower, a nature center, and an 18-hole golf course round out this park's offerings. Peninsula is also the burial site of the last hereditary chief of the Potowatomi Nation, Chief Kahquados, as well as the site of two pioneer cemeteries.

At Peninsula, visitors experience outdoor recreation like fishing (Green Bay is considered one of the most outstanding smallmouth bass fisheries in the Midwest), kayaking, biking, and camping. Birdwatching is another favorite activity. Large tracts of forest, shore, and reclaimed farm land yield diverse species: great blue herons, American redstarts, common yellow-rumped warblers, goshawks, pileated woodpeckers, and wild turkeys.

Petersburg Campground , Georgia

Petersburg has 96 camp sites that are nicely renovated to accommodate large campers, with 86 sites having 50-amp service for the modern RV. All sites are located right on the shoreline of beautiful Thurmond Lake, a 70,000-acre reservoir that provides numerous water-related recreation activities. The wide spacing of camp sites with natural vegetation between sites gives each camper a feeling of having their own private wilderness at their camp site.

Just three miles away is the Thurmond Lake Visitor Center with new displays that feature a sense of being underwater with bubble walls in the entry, windows covered with water graphics, and a boat hanging from the ceiling. There is also a hiking/biking trail that links Petersburg Campground with several other picnic areas along the eight-mile trail. While convenient to I-20 and the Augusta Georgia metropolitan area, Petersburg is far enough away to get a true feeling of nature and getting away from the hustle and bustle of life.

Pfeiffer Big Sur State Park, California

The park has 1,006 acres of redwoods, conifers, oaks, sycamores, cottonwoods, maples, alders, and willows—plus open meadows. Wildlife includes black-tail deer, gray squirrels, raccoons, skunks, and birds such as water ouzels and belted kingfishers. Hikers can enjoy the many scenic trails, including a self-guided nature trail. Some camp sites are along the Big Sur River.

Pocahontas State Park, Virginia

Just 20 miles from downtown Richmond, Pocahontas offers boating, picnicking, camping, hiking, and a wide range of interpretive and environmental education programs. The Aqua Center offers seasonal water-based activities for the entire family, including a kiddie pool, a fountain wet deck, three-foot- and five-foot-deep leisure pools, an activity pool, and two enclosed tube water slides. Rowboat, paddleboat, kayak, and canoe rentals also are available during the summer in the 200-acre Swift Creek Lake. The park's two fishing lakes feature crappie, largemouth bass, bluegill, and catfish.

The park has more than 58 miles of trails throughout 7,724 acres open to hiking, bicycling, and horseback riding. The Civilian Conservation Corps Museum, dedicated to the Depression-era workers who helped build the state park system, is one of a few of its kind in the nation. The park's Heritage Center is available for meetings, events, and seasonal performances. Group area facilities with meeting space and primitive overnight cabins also are available.

Ponderosa State Park, Idaho

Ponderosa State Park covers most of a 1,000-acre peninsula that juts into Payette Lake, just outside McCall. The character of the park is molded by its diverse topography. It ranges from arid sagebrush flats to a lakeside trail; from flat, even ground to steep cliffs; and from dense forest to spongy marsh. Nature trails and dirt roads have been developed so visitors can enjoy these areas. Camping is available in the park and in nearby Lakeview Village.

Prairie Flower Campground, Iowa

Built along the stagecoach road that once connected Fort Des Moines with Polk City, Prairie Flower provides visitors a glimpse of Iowa's once vast prairies. Sprawling over 60 acres, this 248 site campground includes 40 acres of native prairie plantings and boasts picturesque sunsets overlooking Saylorville Lake, a Corps of Engineers project.

Recreation abounds with swimming, fishing, disc golfing, interpretive programs for all ages, exploring the 24-mile paved Neal Smith Trail or nearby Visitor Center and captivating butterfly gardens are just a few. Catch a glimpse of the abundant wildlife and see a bald eagle, osprey, wild turkey, or even a white pelican. Golfers can take a swing at the Tournament Club of Iowa, an Arnold Palmer Signature course just two miles away.

Priest Lake State Park, Idaho

Lying at about 2,400 feet above sea level, Priest Lake State Park has an abundance of beautiful scenery and recreational opportunities. Visitors will enjoy the dense cedar-hemlock forests and the wildlife, such as whitetail deer, black bear, moose and bald eagles. The stately Selkirk Mountain Range towers nearby and numerous streams tumble down the slopes.

Noted for its clear water, Priest Lake extends 19 miles and is connected to the smaller Upper Priest Lake by a placid, two-mile-long water thoroughfare. Steeped in a history of Jesuit priests, Indian villages, homesteaders and logging camps, Priest Lake offers park visitors great diversity ranging from boating and fishing to snowmobiling and cross-country skiing.

Red Fleet State Park, Utah

Red Fleet State Park offers picnic areas, restrooms, boat ramp, sewage disposal, fishing, waterskiing, swimming, dinosaur exhibit, and camping. Camping facilities include 39 campsites, modern restrooms, barbeque grills, covered picnic tables, and fire pits. The campground is located on a hillside, offering a panoramic view of the reservoir and surrounding area. This design is different from most campgrounds. Parking is side-by-side with campsites just a short walk from your vehicle.

Dinosaurs inhabited the land in and around present day Vernal. Red Fleet State Park is home of numerous dinosaur tracks. These tracks are believed to be more than 200 million years old. Paleontologists can tell from these tracks preserved in Navajo sandstone that the dinosaurs were three-toed (tridactyl) and walked on two legs (bipedal). The tracks range from three to 17 inches. A second site of about 40 dinosaur tracks of four to five inches, in the more recent Carmel Formation, has been found in the area, however, the species has not yet been identified.

The tracks can be reached by hiking a 1.25-mile trail that is somewhat strenuous because of its several uphill and downhill sections. The best viewing times of the tracks are early morning or late afternoon. The tracks are somewhat difficult to see when the sun is directly overhead.

Ridgway State Park-Ridgeway, Colorado

Outstanding scenery, ultra-modern facilities, a full-service marina, and magnificent campgrounds beckon visitors to Ridgway State Park. Here you can boat, fish, camp, hike, and study nature in one of the most beautiful areas

in Colorado. Ridgway has 280 camp sites that accommodate trailers, campers, and motor homes. Ridgway is known as one of the nation's most accessible recreation areas for people with disabilities.

Rio Grande Campground, Texas
Located in Big Bend National Park in west Texas, the campground has 100 camping and 25 RV sites. Rio Grande Village is the largest campground in the park, as well as the only one to offer showers and laundry facilities and it is located right on the river. A short nature walk through a wetland area created by a natural spring and dammed up by beaver leads up a hill overlooking the Rio Grande, with the rugged Chisos Mountains rising up in the background.

Amateur naturalists will have a field day here, as over 450 species of birds either live in or migrate through the park. In addition, 75 species of mammals, 56 species of reptiles, and 11 species of amphibians make their home in Big Bend.

Robert W. Craig Campground, West Virginia
Within a winding gorge of the North Branch of the Potomac River, dissected by a plateau with steep and often precipitous slopes rising up from the river channel to high, flat-topped hills, lies Jennings Randolph Lake.

This quiet, secluded lake provides an outdoor sanctuary for this region of northeastern West Virginia and western Maryland. The campground is a highly desired and unspoiled recreation destination.

The campground features an amphitheater, playground, basketball court, horseshoe pits, a mile-long tree identification trail, and a two-mile Sunset Trail offering a panoramic view of the back of the dam and breathtaking sunsets. Evening programs are presented every Saturday evening in the amphitheater starting Memorial Day weekend, catering to family-oriented themes. Hot showers and flush toilets are available in the campground's front camping loop. The campground has 82 camp sites, of which 70 have electrical services.

Roche-A-Cri State Park, Wisconsin

Roche-A-Cri is French, meaning "crevasse in the rock," as described by early explorers. The park includes prairie and oak woodland and surrounds an intriguing sandstone mound 300 feet high, and the smaller Chickadee Rock. Visitors can climb 303 steps to the top of Roche-A-Cri Mound for panoramic views of the ancient landscape. At the accessible rock art observation area, visitors can see and learn about petroglyphs and pictographs. This is the only accessible rock art site for the public in Wisconsin.

Roche-A-Cri is a quiet, family campground with 41 rustic camp sites. Visitors can hike on six miles of trails, picnic, fish in Carter Creek or near-by Friendship Lake, watch wildlife like turkeys, deer, and turkey vultures circling the mound, and cross-country ski in winter. The annual Pumpkin Walk is held before Halloween and features games and haunted hayrides through the campground. Naturalist programs are held on weekends during the summer.

Salisbury Beach State Reservation, Massachussets.

This 521-acre park is just south of the New Hampshire border and stretches for 3.8 miles along the Atlantic Ocean. There are over-the-dune boardwalks, a new playground, and a pavilion on the beach. There are two boat ramps that access the Merrimack River, as well as interpretive programs and a nature center. Campers stay busy fishing, swimming, and boating. The campground has 484 camp sites with flush toilets, showers, dumping station, and electrical and water hook-ups. It's open from mid-April to mid-October.

The Salisbury Reservation is only 45 miles from Boston and within an hour's ride of the White Mountains. The combination of oceanside beach, riverfront, estuary, and salt marsh provide visitors with a wide variety of recreational opportunities which include swimming, picnicking, beach combing, birdwatching, and fishing. The three beach bathhouses are universally accessible, two have shade shelters, and all have an elevated boardwalk leading to the ocean beach.

Salt Point State Park, California

Rocky promontories, panoramic views, kelp-dotted coves, and the dramatic sounds of pounding surf; open grasslands, forested hills, pristine prairies, and pygmy forests—you can experience all of these coastal wonders within the 6,000 acres of Salt Point State Park. With 20 miles of hiking trails, over six miles of rugged coastline, and an underwater park, you can enjoy a variety of picnicking, hiking, horseback riding, fishing, skin and SCUBA diving, and camping.

Salthouse Branch Park, Virginia

Canoeing on crystal-clear waters surrounded by the Blue Ridge Mountains; watching the reflection of the changing leaves in the fall—these are just a couple of scenarios offered by Salthouse Branch. Deer, black bears, wild turkey, quail, and ruffed grouse all call this area home. Beaver, muskrat, and wood, mallard, and black ducks live peacefully in and along the shores of Philpott Lake, which is also home to large and small mouth bass, walleye, bluegill, crappie, and catfish. The Smith River below the dam is known throughout the country for its great trout fishing.

Some of the amenities at the campground include hot showers, two swimming beaches, a new amphitheatre where park rangers present various interpretive programs, water and electric sites, boat ramp and courtesy dock, hiking trail, and beautiful picnic areas. With over 93 camp sites, camping opportunities are always plentiful.

Santee State Park, South Carolina

Headquarters for outdoor enthusiasts and nature lovers of all kinds from its ideal location near Interstates 95 and 26, the 2,500-acre park is located on the south shore of Lake Marion, nationally known for its fishing.

Santee State Park has two campgrounds with a total of 163 sites. Each site is packed sand and has individual water and electrical hook-ups and picnic table. Many sites accommodate RVs up to 40 feet. Both campgrounds are convenient to restroom facilities with hot showers. Laundry facilities are also located on site.

The park has one 7.5-mile biking/hiking trail and three nature/walking trails. Lakes Marion and Moultrie are nationally known for their fishing, especially for largemouth bass, striped bass, bream, crappie, and catfish. Two boat ramps, one that is handicap-accessible, provide private boat access to Lake Marion for recreation.

Scusset Beach State Reservation, Massachussets

Just one hour from Boston and at the foot of the bridge that leads to Cape Cod, Scusset Beach offers 380 acres to explore, including miles of ocean beach. It offers swimming and fishing, interpretive programs, and beautiful views of the Atlantic Ocean and the Cape Cod Canal.

There are 103 camp sites, five for tents and 98 for RVs. Camp sites feature flush toilets, showers, dumping station, and electrical and water hookups. It's open from late April to mid October.

South Sandusky Campground, Illinois

Nestled on the southern shore of Sandusky Cove lies Rend Lake's peaceful South Sandusky campground. With easy access to Interstate 57, it is both a popular overnight stopover site for travelers and a destination campground for families. There are 120 camp sites, consisting of sites with full hook-ups, 50- or 30-amp electric service only, and non-electric walk-in tent sites. Two shower buildings with hot showers and several flush comfort stations are located throughout the campground.

The campground is located on the lake, with some sites overlooking Sandusky Cove, a designated no-wake cove popular with anglers and pleasure boaters alike. Campers are welcome to fish along the shoreline and moor their boats on the shoreline during their stay. A scenic paved bike trail runs through the campground and provides access to a public beach, Rend Lake Marina, and the Dam West recreation area. The Blackberry Nature Trail is not far from the entrance.

Steamboat Lake State Park, Colorado

Nestled at the base of majestic Hahn's Peak in northern Colorado, Steamboat Lake offers breathtaking scenery and plenty of excellent recreational opportunities. One of the most popular areas in the state, Steamboat Lake is a park for all seasons.

Most of the 188 camp sites at Steamboat Lake are well shaded by aspen or lodgepole pine, and many sites are near the shoreline. Camp sites include level parking areas, table/fire ring pads, and 14 X14 tent pads. Electrical hook-ups, showers, and laundry and dump station facilities are also available.

Tolland State Forest, Massachussets

The most notable feature at Tolland is the 1,200 acre reservoir, the largest recreational lake in western Massachusetts. The campground resides on a lovely peninsula that extends into the reservoir. Visitors can swim, motor boat, water ski, canoe, fish, hike, mountain bike and participate in interpretive programs.

Tub Run Recreation Area, Pennsylvania

Come to the great outdoors in the heart of the Laurel Highlands in southwestern Pennsylvania, where Tub Run Campground is located in a quiet cove at Youghiogheny River Lake, surrounded by lush forested hillsides. Known as a favorite spot for campers with boats, the campground offers a variety of camping opportunities with its 101 sites, including walk-in tent-only sites, standard, and electric sites. Campers may choose among several camp site locations, from alongside shaded Tub Run, under the trees in the wooded walk-in tent area, or close to the lake and swim beach. Each camp site is outfitted with a table, fire ring, and lantern holder.

Accommodations include modern restrooms, hot showers, playground, dump station, launch ramp, mooring peninsula, and swim beach. Campers have ready access to recreational opportunities on the lake, including fishing, boating, swimming, and other water sports. Reservations are available during the recreation season mid-May through mid-September.

Twin Lakes Campground, South Carolina

Located south of Clemson University and 10 minutes from Interstate 85 in the "Golden Corner" of South Carolina, Twin Lakes, on Hartwell Lake, offers excellent opportunities to enjoy fishing, swimming, boating, and watching wildlife. The 56,000 acres of water and the 20,450 acres of public lands at Hartwell Lake provide the perfect setting for family outdoor activities.

The campground has102 camp sites with electric and water hook-ups, a day-use area with two shelters with electricity, and individual picnic sites with picnic tables and grills. The adjacent boat ramp has two launching lanes and over 75 boat parking spaces.

The nearby 7,000-acre Fants Grove Wildlife Management has 15 miles of trails for hunting, hiking, or mountain biking. More trails especially popular for mountain biking are within a short 15-minute drive to the Issaqueena Trail system that offers an additional 25 miles of intermediate trails.

Wasatch Mountain State Park, Utah

The park provides year-round recreation, including camping, picnicking, hiking, golf, snowmobiling, off-highway vehicle use, and horseback riding. Park facilities include 139 camping/picnicking areas, two group-use pavilions, modern restrooms, hot showers and utility hookups. The chalet, a ranch-style building complete with kitchen facilities, is available for summer and winter group outings. The primitive Little Deer Creek campground is an excellent area for summer group parties and reunions.

Wasatch Mountain State Park was proud host of the 2002 Olympic Winter Games at Soldier Hollow. The venue remains open to the public year-round with a variety of activities and events. Soldier Hollow offers cross-country skiing, tubing, summer and winter biathlon, in-line skating facilities, and more.

Wasatch Mountain State Park offers picnic areas, camping facilities, and ADA accessible restrooms with showers, sewage disposal, group pavilion, visitor center, golf course, full-service pro shop, driving range, concessionaire, hiking, cross-country skiing, and snowmobiling.

Watkins Glen State Park, New York

If you listen hard enough during the summer months you can hear the roar of the Watkins Glen International Race Course from Watkins Glen State Park. The campground has 305 wooded camp sites (53 of which are electric), playgrounds, basketball courts, and planned recreation programs. The nearby lakes and creeks are ideal for fishing and renowned for the annual spring run of rainbow trout.

Hikers can walk along the winding paths of the historic gorge. Glen Creek has poured down the glacially steepened valley side for 12,000 years and has left 19 glistening waterfalls and cascades. The wearing away of shale rock found within some of the cliffs allows hikers to walk behind some of the waterfalls.

Wells State Park, Massachussets
Wells is a quiet campground nestled on a hillside adjacent to Walker Pond. The park offers mountain biking, boating, fishing, swimming, hiking and interpretive programs. The park is convenient to the very popular Old Sturbridge Village. Wells has a laid back, peaceful feeling and with a location near the MA Turnpike offers many opportunities for sight seeing, exploring and relaxing.

Willard Bay State Park, Utah
Willard Bay is a freshwater reservoir located 12 miles northwest of Ogden on the flood plains of the Great Salt Lake. An earth filled dike and natural

shoreline make up the 20-mile enclosures. Recently renovated, the park offers state-of-the-art day-use and camping facilities, boat launch ramps, and group-use areas.

Cottonwood Campground is located at the North Marina and provides full hookups (water, sewer, electricity) for RVs. There are 39 campsites, sixteen of which are open year-round. All sites are available April 1 through October 30. Each campsite has a barbeque grill, fire ring and picnic table on a cement pad. Tents can be accommodated, but there are not many good spots for a tent. There are two modern restrooms with flush toilets and showers. Large Cottonwood trees dominate the landscape providing adequate shade. Reservations are highly recommended for this campground. No sites are held for first-come, first-serve.

Winhall Brook Campground, Vermont

Winhall Brook is nestled in the Green Mountains along the Winhall Brook and the West River near Jamaica, Vermont. The rural setting of this campground has a strong appeal to the outdoorsman at heart. The campground has a lean-to's, dump station, electric and water hook-ups, hot showers, weekend interpretative programs, and eight miles of hiking/biking trails. Two miles of the West River Trail, which follows the old West River Rail Roadbed, are wheelchair accessible.

The campground is also located near the Green Mountain National Forest and the Appalachian and Long Trails. The campground is open for the spring and fall white water releases from Ball Mountain Dam. Facilities include a laundromat, convenience stores, and a Thrill Park, alpine slide, water slide, devil carts, and mini-golf, located within seven miles of the park.

Chapter 4: Camping Recipes

Breakfast

Campfire Muffins

6 oranges
2 packages of muffin mix
Cut oranges in half and scoop out orange segments (it is the hollowed peel shells that you need, but keep the fruit for use with fruit salad or juice). Prepare the muffin mix according to the package directions. Fill the orange-peel cups half full with batter. Wrap each one loosely with heavy-duty aluminum foil. Place in hot coals and make certain the batter side stays up. Cook 5–10 minutes, until muffins are done.

Breakfast Sandwiches

Bacon, ham or sausage
Scrambled eggs (any ingredients you like with your eggs)
2 slices of bread/person
1 slice of cheese/person
Before leaving on your camping trip, cook enough meat for the number of people you'll be serving. Let it cool, and wrap up. Using a microwave egg cooker, mix eggs and cook into little egg patties, then seal in a container. On the camp site, butter a cast iron pie maker. Add two slices of bread, your choice of breakfast meat, an egg patty and a slice of cheese. Cook in the campfire until done. Please let cool, as the cheese can be extremely hot!

Bagged Breakfast Omelet

Eggs (1–2 per person)
Milk
Cheese
Ham
Bacon
Onions
Peppers
Tomatoes
Mushrooms
Cayenne
Pita Pocket Bread (Optional)
Zip-tight freezer bag
Beat eggs, put in bag with desired amount of milk. Add some or all additional ingredients. Seal the bag tightly. Then place bag in boiling water and cook for 3–5 minutes until cooked to your preference. To eat as a breakfast sandwich, put egg combination in pita bread.

Scrambled Tortillas

Eggs (2 per person)
Bacon (2–3 slices per person)
Shredded Cheese (combo recommended)
Salsa (optional)
Peppers (red, green, or hot)
Flour tortillas
Cook bacon in skillet and lay on paper towels to absorb grease. Scramble eggs in the same skillet where bacon was cooked. You may want to drain the remaining bacon grease left in the skillet. If preferred, warm tortillas by wrapping them in foil and warming them over the fire; be sure not to warm too long as they can burn. Place the scrambled eggs, bacon, cheese, salsa, and desired peppers in the tortillas. Then roll it up like you would a burrito and devour.

Breakfast Corncakes

1 pkg. corn muffin mix
1 egg
2 tbsp. melted shortening
3/4 cup milk
Pancake batter (follow directions to prepare this separately)
Mix ingredients together. Spoon desired size of mixture onto a hot greased griddle. Be sure to turn pancakes when bubbles appear. Serve with your favorite breakfast meat.

Fruit Pancakes

1 pkg. of preferred fruit muffin mix
1 egg
2 tbsp. melted shortening
3/4 cup milk
Pancake batter
Mix ingredients together. Spoon desired size of mixture onto a hot greased griddle. Be sure to turn pancakes when bubbles appear.

Fresh Berry Pancakes

Freshly picked blackberries, black raspberries, elderberries, etc.
Sugar
Pancake mix
Milk
Eggs
Water
Pick fresh berries from the wild (check with the park you are staying at for regulations) and sprinkle sugar to taste on them. Make pancakes and spread fruit over the top and eat up.

Monte Cristo Sandwich Twist

1 egg
Dash of milk

2 slices of bread
2 slices of ham
2 slices of turkey
2 slices of American cheese
Raspberry jelly
Powdered sugar

Mix the egg and milk together and spread on both sides of bread. Place the meat and cheese between the bread and place in your non-stick iron pie maker. Cook for about 2–3 minutes. Sprinkle with powdered sugar and dip in raspberry jelly. Delicious!

Peanut Butter and Jelly Cinnamon Sugar French Toast

2 slices of bread
Peanut butter
Jelly
1/4 cup milk
2 eggs, beaten
Icing sugar or brown sugar
Cinnamon

Beat eggs, add milk. Spread the peanut butter and jelly on 2 slices of bread. Put together like sandwich. Dip into egg mixture. Place in non-stick pie iron maker and place in hot coals for around 4–6 minutes. Toast to desired preference. Serve with powdered sugar or cinnamon.

Morning Campfire Breakfast

1 pound bacon or preferred breakfast meat
1/2 cup chopped onion
1/2 cup chopped green/red pepper
Small can chopped mushrooms
1 dozen eggs
Shredded Cheese
Cayenne
Salt and pepper

Cut bacon into pieces and put into large cast-iron skillet on the campfire.

Cook until it's half-way done, add chopped onion, pepper, mushrooms. Stir until bacon is crisp and vegetables are tender. Then beat eggs in large bowl, adding a little water, and stir into bacon mixture in skillet. Stir constantly until eggs are set. Serve with shredded cheese, season to taste.

Ultimate Breakfast Casserole

1 tube of crescent rolls
1 lb. cooked bacon, ham, or sausage, drained
Fresh mushrooms, sliced
Fresh peppers, diced
6 eggs, beaten
3/4 lb. cheese combination
1 can of cream of onion or broccoli soup
Line a 13 x 9-inch oven dish with rolls. Layer the oven dish with sausage, mushrooms, and half of the cheese combination. Mix eggs and soup and pour over casserole. Sprinkle remaining cheese on top. Chill overnight. Bake at 350 for 1 hour.

Cinnamon Vanilla Twist French Toast

1 egg
5 egg whites
1 cup of low fat or skim milk
2 tbsp. sugar
1 tbsp. vanilla extract
1 tsp. of cinnamon
Powdered sugar (optional)
8 slices of white or whole-wheat bread
Combine and whisk together eggs, milk, sweetener, vanilla extract, and cinnamon in a medium bowl. Spray pan or griddle with non-stick spray. Preheat at medium to medium-high heat. Soak the bread slices in egg mixture until moistened. Place bread slice on griddle or frying pan. Grill until bottom of bread is browned and then flip with spatula to the other side. Serve warm with sprinkled cinnamon and powdered sugar.

Campfire Oatmeal

1/2 cup of oatmeal
2 sweeteners
1 cup water
3 medium sliced strawberries
Cinnamon
Mix oatmeal, sweeteners, and boiled water together. Add slices of strawberries and enjoy!

Fresh Fruit Cottage Cheese

1 cup low-fat cottage cheese
1 cup sliced strawberries
1 cup of blueberries or raspberries
1 cup diced pineapple
2 packages of sweetener
Mix all ingredients together in a bowl.

Toasted TMO Sandwiches

4 large tomatoes
2 large onions
Sliced bread
Butter/margarine
Mayonnaise
Salt and pepper
Butter the bread, and slice up the tomatoes and onions. Place between 2 slices of bread and season with salt and pepper. Place sandwiches in a pie iron and place on coals until toasted.

Sausage and Egg English Muffins

1 lb. sausage patties
8–10 eggs
2 tbsp. milk
Shredded cheese

Butter or vegetable spray
Salt and pepper to taste
1 pkg. English muffins, cut in half
Butter or spray side of muffin, put butter side toward iron, layer sausage patty, a little egg (it will run but set when cooked), shredded cheese, and top with other muffin half. Cook over campfire until sausage and egg are set.

All-in-One Campfire Breakfast

4 large potatoes
1 medium onion
6 slices cooked peameal bacon or 12 strips of cooked bacon
3 eggs
1 cup milk
1 cup shredded cheddar or other cheese
Olive oil
Large tin/aluminum baking pan with tin foil
Cut potatoes into small cubes or thin slices and dice onion into small pieces. Whisk eggs and milk together. If bacon is not already cooked, cook in pan and drain any excess fat. In large baking pan, place the potatoes and onions. Pour egg and milk mixture over the potatoes evenly, and spread half of the bacon pieces over top. Add shredded cheese and remaining bacon as the top layer and cover baking dish with tin foil.
Place pan over campfire cooking rack and cook for approx. 30–40 minutes. Monitor campfire to ensure heat source is evenly spread, otherwise only half of the dish may be cooked properly. When ready, remove tin foil and serve!

Rising Sun Eggs 'n' Toast

4 slices of your favorite bread
4 eggs
4 slices of ham or Canadian bacon
4 slices of cheese
Use warm heat for your pan and add some oil or butter. Pressa glass or mug down on the bread until it punches a hole in the middle of the bread. Place the bread on your pan and toast lightly on both sides. If your pan is large

enough do two slices at the same time. Crack an egg into the hole in the bread and cook until the egg is turning white. Flip the bread over, and add some cheese to the other side. Also warm the ham or cook the bacon on the side of the pan until they are ready and the cheese is melted. The egg will look like a rising sun in the center of the bread and you can add designs for kids for more fun at breakfast.

Snacks

Snack Mix

1/2 cup each of:
Unsalted sesame sticks
Cajun sesame sticks
Pumpkin seeds
Pine nuts
Soy nuts
Unsalted peanuts
Hulled sunflower seeds
Almonds
Brazil nuts
Macadamia nuts
Any grain cereal
Preheat oven to 350 degrees F. Mix all ingredients together in a large bowl and add seasoning salt, pepper and cayenne for added spice. Bake for 5 min and remove. Allow to cool Seal in plastic bag and it's ready to eat on your trip.

Camper's Trail Mix

Peanuts
Raisins
Dried cranberry
Dried pineapple
Chocolate covered raisins/peanuts
Dried papaya
Coconut flakes

Cashews
Sunflower seeds (hulled)
Banana chips
Pretzel sticks
Mix together in a container and serve. You can add any dry ingredient you wish that may add to this delicious camper's mix.

Mexi-tater Camper Style

1 medium to large-sized potato
Taco seasoning
Cayenne
Salt and pepper
Shredded cheese
Poke holes in potato with fork and wrap in foil. Cook over the fire on grill. When done cut open and spoon out meat of potato and mash in a separate bowl. Add some taco seasoning, cayenne, salt, and pepper, and mix together well. Place mashed potato back in potato half and serve with shredded cheese.

Camp Chili Roasted Peanuts

1 1/2 tbsp. olive oil
1/2 tbsp. crushed chilies
1/4 tbsp. cayenne
1 tbsp. cumin
1/4 tbsp. turmeric
1 tbsp. sugar
3 cups salted peanuts
Preheat oven to 325F. Combine all ingredients except peanuts in baking pan and mix well. Add peanuts and toss. Spread mixture out in a single layer and bake for 20–25 minutes. Cool and serve.

Cracker Jack Caramel Corn

2 cups of peanuts
4 cups popped popcorn

1 cup of butter/margarine (melted)
2 cups of brown sugar
1/2 cup of corn syrup
1/2 tsp. salt
1/2 tsp. baking powder

Preheat oven to 250F. In large bowl mix the popcorn and peanuts. In a large saucepan, combine butter, sugar, corn syrup and salt. Boil for 5 minutes and remove from heat. Add baking powder. Pour over popcorn mix and stir with wooden spoon. Spread out mixture onto baking sheet and bake in oven for one hour, stirring occasionally. Cool, break up, and enjoy!

Cinnamon Sugar Almonds

3 egg whites
4 tsp. cold water
5 cups almonds
3/4 cup sugar or substitute
1/2 tsp. salt
3 tbsp. cinnamon
Non-stick cooking spray

Preheat oven to 250F. Spray a cookie sheet with non-stick cooking spray. In a bowl combine egg whites and water and whip together. Add almonds and stir, making sure almonds are covered. In a separate bowl combine sugar, salt, and cinnamon. Mix well. Sprinkle over almonds and mix well. Bake for 50–60 minutes. Cool and serve.

Crunchy Camper Taco Dip

1/2 cup sour cream
1/2 cup cream cheese
1 cup salsa
1 pouch taco seasoning mix
Shredded cheese
Jalapeno peppers (Optional)
Tortilla chips

Combine and mix in a large bowl the sour cream and cream cheese; blend well. Stir in taco seasoning. In a pie dish, layer starting with sour cream mixture followed by salsa, repeating until mixture is gone. Top with shredded cheese and serve with tortilla chips. For added spice slice up some jalapenos and place on top of dip.

Peanut Butter Mallo Sandwich

Loaf of bread
Butter/margarine, softened
Peanut butter
Marshmallows or mallow spread
Pie iron

Butter one side of each bread slice Spread peanut butter on one slice and mallow spread on another slice and make sandwich. Place sandwich buttered side down in pie iron. Cook over fire in pie iron until bread is golden brown. Be careful—filling will be very hot.

Healthy Yogurt Camp Mix

Raw oats or pre-mixed flavored instant oatmeal
1 large container of yogurt (any flavor)
Fresh fruit bits (banana slices, melon, berries, etc.)
Mix together and enjoy!

Baked Campfire Apples

1 apple per person
Brown sugar
Raisins
Dried fruit
Nuts

Core apple three-quarters of the way, leaving bottom in. Fill the center with your choice of raisins, nuts, and dried fruit mixed with a little bit of brown sugar. Wrap apple in foil and place over hot coals for 15–20 minutes.

Campfire Ants on a Log

Celery sticks
Peanut butter/cheese spread
Raisins
Wash the celery and cut it into pieces about six inches long. Spread peanut butter or cheese over the entire length of the celery. Press raisins into peanut butter/cheese.

Pineapple Campfire Rings

1 can pineapple slices
Marshmallows
Roasting sticks
Skewer the pineapple slices, working a marshmallow into the center hole. Toast over a low fire or on a grill until the pineapple gets hot and the marshmallow browns.

Camp Ham Party Ball

1 can flaked ham
1 pkg. cream cheese, softened
1/2 tsp. salt
1 tbsp. lemon juice
2 tsp. grated onion
1/2 cup chopped pecans
3 tsp. chopped parsley
Drain water from ham and remove from can. Break up ham in bowl, combine with cream cheese, salt, lemon juice, and grated onion; blend well together. Roll into a ball and roll in a bowl of pecans and parsley to cover. Chill for 2–3 hours and serve.

Lunch

Camper Fish and Chips

Medium-size potato
1 tbsp. of olive oil
Salt and pepper
Onion powder
Garlic powder
Halibut
Tartar sauce
Malt vinegar

Slice potato in to thin strips. Place halibut and potato on foil square lightly greased with olive oil. Sprinkle with salt, pepper, onion powder, and garlic powder. Seal foil into packet and cook over camp grill for 25–30 minutes until fish and chips are cooked. Serve with malt vinegar and tartar sauce.

Dough Boys

Hot dog weiners (beef, chicken, turkey)
Crescent roll dough

Separate crescent dough and wrap individual hot dogs with the dough. Using a hot dog stick or fork, cook over hot coals until dough is light brown. Serve with your favorite condiments.

Deluxe Campfire Pizza

1 pkg. large pita pocket bread
1 can or bottle of pizza sauce
3 slices salami
2 slices bacon, cut into small pieces
1 pkg. shredded mozzarella cheese
Sliced veggies (onions, peppers, mushroom, zucchini)

Spread pitas with pizza sauce, sprinkle cheese on top. Place meat and veggies on top, place on foil over campfire grill (make sure the flame is not too high) or on top of low flame, barbeque for about 10 minutes or until cheese is melted and bacon is cooked through, and enjoy.

Cheesy Tortillas

Flour tortillas
Shredded cheese
Onions
Peppers
Mushrooms
Bacon
Warm a flour tortilla in a pan. When warm add cheese. Add desired veggies and meat and fold tortilla like a burrito and enjoy.

Pie Iron Pizza Sandwiches

2 pieces of bread
Pizza sauce
Mozzarella cheese
Pepperoni
Preferred pizza toppings
Butter each piece of bread on one side. Place one piece of bread in one half of the pie iron cooker with the buttered side out. Place the sauce, cheese, and other pizza ingredients in the middle of the bread and place the second piece of bread over the top, buttered side out. Now clamp the cooker together and lock it. Place the cooker in the hot coals and rotate when you think one side is done.

Beans and Hot Dog Pieces

4 cans of beans (maple syrup–flavored)
10 strips of bacon
1 onion, diced
1/4 cup of water
12 all-beef hot dogs, sliced crosswise
1/4 cup of maple syrup
Cook bacon in skillet and empty most of the grease (leave some so the remaining ingredients don't stick). Place diced onions in skillet, cook until onions are transparent. Add water. Combine beans and cook over campfire until hot, then add hotdog pieces and syrup in the last few minutes of cooking.

Campfire Cottage Fries

4 potatoes, cut into thin or large strips
Salt, pepper, garlic powder and cayenne for spice
1 green pepper, sliced
1 onion, sliced
Butter-flavored cooking spray
Spray a large square of heavy duty foil with buttered-flavor cooking spray. Place potato strips, green pepper and onion on the foil dull side out. Sprinkle with salt, pepper, garlic powder, and cayenne. Shake a bit to coat. Seal the foil, leaving a steam vent on top. Grill over hot coals turning several times until potatoes are tender, about 30–45 minutes.

Cajun Meat Burgers

2 tbsp. water
2 tsp. hot sauce
1/2 lb. ground pork/beef/chicken
1/2 lb. bulk hot sausage
4 sandwich buns
4 lettuce leaves
Tomatoes, sliced
Heat up the grill and in a large bowl, combine water and hot sauce; blend well. Add preferred meat and sausage, mix gently. Shape into 4 patties. Place on grill, over medium heat. Cook 14 minutes or until no longer pink, turning once. Serve on buns with lettuce leaves and tomatoe slices, as well as your desired burger ingredients.

Smoked Turkey and Honey Apple Sandwiches

1/4 cup Dijonaise creamy mustard blend
2 tbsp. honey
8 slices seven-grain or whole wheat bread
1 cup shredded cheddar cheese
1/2 lb. sliced/shaved smoked turkey
1 apple (cored and thinly sliced)
In a small bowl combine mustard blend and honey; spread on one side of

each slice of bread. Layer cheese on 4 bread slices; top with turkey, apple and remaining bread. Cut sandwiches in half.

Sweet Potato Crisps

1 large sweet potato
1 large egg white; whipped
1/2 tsp. vanilla extract
1/4 tsp. sweetener
1/4 tsp. cinnamon
Preheat oven to 425°F. Slice the sweet potato on a mandolin to ensure thin, even slices. Place slices into a bag or plastic container with a top, making sure there's a little room. Add remaining ingredients and shake up to coat well. Spread coated slices over lightly greased cooking sheet. Sprinkle additional sweetener and cinnamon to ensure a tasty colorful coating. Bake at 425°F for approximately 25 minutes until browned.

Campfire Chicken Wings

1 lb. of wings
Coat with a mixture of hot sauce and oil
Barbeque until crispy and serve with blue cheese dressing, celery sticks, and LOTS of napkins!

Cheese-Stuffed Burgers

Ground beef
Shredded cheese
Salt and pepper
Garlic salt
Bacon
Tomato slices
Buns
Form medium-size meatballs and then stuff with cheese. Once this is done, flatten into

patties. Season the patties with salt, pepper, and garlic salt and then cook over fire. In a small skillet or foil pack, cook the bacon. Put this and the remaining ingredients on a nicely toasted bun, and you have a great burger.

Grilled Tuna Salad Sandwich

1 can of tuna or salmon
Mayonnaise
Salt and pepper
Onion powder
Green and red peppers, diced
8 slices of bread
4 or 5 eggs
Butter
Combine tuna/salmon with mayonnaise, salt and pepper, and onion powder and add in diced green and red peppers. Mix well. Spread between two pieces of bread. Melt a pat of butter in pan, dip sandwich in eggs and place in pan. Cook like french toast.

Spicy Egg Salad Sandwiches

8 hard-boiled eggs; chopped
1/2 cup mayonnaise
1 tbsp. Dijon mustard
Salt and pepper
1/4 cup chopped celery (optional)
1 small onion, chopped (optional)
1 dash paprika or cayenne (optional)
Sliced bread
Combine all desired ingredients in bowl and serve between two slices of bread.

Spicy and Sweet Mango Cucumber Salad

1 cucumber, peeled, seeded, diced
1 mango, peeled and diced
1–2 tbsp. lime juice

1–2 tbsp. lemon juice
1/2 tsp. chili peppers, minced
1 small red pepper, minced
2 tbsp. dried shredded coconut
2 tsp. brown sugar
Combine all ingredients in a large bowl. Mix well and serve.

Gourmet Macaroni and Cheese

1 box macaroni and cheese (with the premixed cheese sauce)
1 can tuna, drained
1 celery stalk, chopped
1/2 onion, diced
Salt and pepper to taste
Boil water over campfire or camp stove in pot. Cook macaroni until tender. Add packet of cheese, dump in can of tuna, chopped celery, diced onion, add salt and pepper, and stir. To really add some flavor, add some shredded cheese if available.

Stuffed Cheese Dogs

Hot dogs
Cheese (any type of block cheese except processed will do)
Bacon (5–6 slices per hot dog.)
Cut a slit down the center of the hot dog, but not all the way through. Place a thick slice of cheese in the center of the hot dog. Wrap the hot dog with the bacon strips firmly, securing with toothpicks (be sure to cover the entire hot dog so that the cheese does not run out when cooking). Cook over the campfire until ready. Cook the side with the cheese first and then rotate and cook the other side. This way when the cheese melts, you will have rotated the cheese right side up, so that it won't all drip out.

Dinner

Campfire Foil Salmon

2 salmon steaks
2 tbsp. butter or margarine
1 lemon and 1 lime (save the lemon to juice over fish)
2–4 garlic cloves, finely chopped
Salt and fresh ground pepper and cayenne for added spice
1–2 tsp. of cumin

Combine butter with lemon or lime juice, garlic, salt, pepper, cayenne, and cumin. Salt and pepper salmon and place on a sheet of foil. Spread butter mixture on salmon and create foil pouch. Cook on grill over fire until fish flakes easily. Squeeze lemon over salmon. Serve with desired vegetables.

Pizza Sauce Potatoes

Butter
6 potatoes, sliced
Pizza sauce
Pepperoni
Shredded cheese
Any other toppings of your choice

On a heavy piece of aluminum foil, put down sliced pieces of butter. Then a layer of sliced potatoes. Then add some sauce, cheese, pepperoni and your toppings. Continue to make layers until all is used. Fold up and close one end. Add about 1/4 cup of water and seal other end. Cook over campfire grill for about 30–35 minutes.

Campfire Chicken Clambake

4 cups water
1 cup vinegar
Potatoes, sliced
Chicken wings
Sausage

Corn on the cob
Shrimp
Onions
Cherrystone clams

Take a large pot, such as a turkey fryer. Start at bottom with 4 cups of water, 1 cup of vinegar then in layers potatoes, chicken wings, sausage, corn on the cob and in husk, shrimp, onions, and top off with clams. Cook for 1 hour and add each item every accordingly every 10 minutes. Serve and enjoy!

Campfire Stew

1 lb. ground beef/pork/chicken
1 small onion
Garlic salt (as desired)
Pepper (as desired.)
1 can vegetable or onion soup

In a large heavy pot, brown ground meat with onion, garlic salt and pepper. When meat is no longer pink add can of soup, simmer, and serve.

Campfire Chicken Pita Pockets

4 boneless, skinless chicken breast halves
1 cup of Greek salad dressing
4 pita pocket breads
1 bag of mixed salad
Ranch salad dressing or desired chicken dressing

Marinade chicken breast in Greek salad dressing in a zip-tight bag for 1 hour. Place chicken on hot grill over low flamed campfire. Cook for 20–30 minutes or until juices run clear. Remove chicken and let cool. Cut chicken into pieces. Fill pitas with salad and chicken and top with ranch or preferred dressing.

Lemon Camp Chicken

1 whole chicken—3–4 lbs. is good.
1 whole lemon
Vegetable oil

Variety of spices: salt, pepper, garlic, onion salt, basil, oregano, Italian seasoning, cayenne, paprika

Clean and skin chicken, cut lemon into quarters and place inside of chicken cavity, rub and coat entire chicken with oil, and season with desired spices. Place chicken on a cooking rack. Preheat your grill to 350 degrees, place chicken inside and cover. Cook for 45 minutes to 1 hour.

Campfire Kabobs

1 lb. diced meat beef/chicken/pork/lamb
Italian salad dressing
Bell pepper (any color)
Onion
Zucchini (green or yellow)
Cherry tomatoes
Mushrooms
1 can whole potatoes, drained
Seasoning Salt and pepper
Wooden skewers

Place meat in a zip-tight bag and add enough salad dressing to cover meat. Allow meat to marinade for several hours. Keep in cooler or fridge while marinating. If using wooden skewers, place skewers in water and allow to soak (prevents burning). Cut bell pepper, onion and zucchini into bite-size pieces. Put pieces of meat and vegetables on skewers, alternating between meat and vegetables. Pour remaining salad dressing over kabobs. Sprinkle with seasoning salt and pepper. Cook on the grill until meat is done.

Mac and Cheese Supreme

1 can condensed cheddar cheese soup
1/2 soup can of milk
1/2 soup can of water
1 cup macaroni (uncooked)
Combine and mix soup, milk and water in a pan. Bring to a boil. Stir in macaroni. Cook over low heat for approximately 10 minutes, or until macaroni is cooked.

Pita Pocket Pizza

4 pieces of pita pocket bread
2 cups of pizza sauce
2 cups of shredded cheese
Aluminum foil
Pizza toppings of choice
Choose pizza toppings of your choice (mushrooms, green peppers, sausage, pepperoni etc.). Slice pita pocket bread three quarters of the way through. Spread pizza sauce on the bottom layer of the pita pocket bread. Put in toppings and sprinkle with shredded cheese. Close and wrap the pita and wrap inside foil. Cook over coals until hot for 15–20 minutes.

Salsa Chicken

4 boneless, skinless chicken breast halves
1 container gourmet salsa
Seasoning salt and pepper
Wrap each piece of chicken into a foil envelope with salsa, seal foil tightly.

Place on grill over fire and cook for 40 minutes. Or place on a rock near the fire, not directly in the flames and cook for the same amount of time, turning every 10–15 minutes.

Dinner Wrap

1 piece heavy-duty aluminum foil
Vegetables of choice (potatoes, mushrooms, onion, pepper, carrots), diced
Meat of choice (boneless and cubed)
Seasoning of choice
Butter
1 cup of water
Place all ingredients in the center of the aluminum foil. Fold edges tightly, leaving one end open. Pour water into folded wrap and tightly fold the open end. Then place the wrap directly on coals. Cook for 30 minutes turning every 10 minutes. Vegetables should be tender and meat juices should run clear.

Campfire Goulash

Ground beef/pork/chicken
1 jar of tomato sauce
Green pepper, diced
Mushrooms, sliced
Onion, diced
8 oz. macaroni, uncooked
Cook ground meat until no longer pink. Drain the grease. Add in jar of tomato sauce, green peppers, mushrooms and onion. Add macaroni. Keep adding water until macaroni is cooked.

Italian Grilled Chicken

Skinless chicken breasts
Italian salad dressing
Place chicken and Italian salad dressing in a zip-tight bag. Marinate in fridge for 3 hours or longer. Cook on grill 10 minutes each side until juices run clear.

Camp Mexican-Style Rice

1/2 lb. ground beef/pork/chicken
1 small onion, chopped
18 oz. can Mexican seasoned tomatoes
3/4 cup Minute rice
18 oz. can kidney beans
1/2 cup water

Cook ground meat with the onions until no pink remains in meat. Drain the grease, then add tomatoes, rice, beans, and water. Bring to a boil. Cover. Let stand for 5 minutes. Serve with flour tortillas or tortilla chips.

Campfire Stuffed Tomatoes

Tomatoes
Sliced cheese
Canned tuna, salmon or chicken
Italian-style breadcrumbs
Butter

Spoon out some of the meat of a tomato. Place one slice of cheese in tomato. Fill with canned tuna or chicken or salmon. Top with Italian breadcrumbs. Put a piece of butter on top. Wrap in foil. Cook on coals until cheese is melted.

Cajun Campfire Shrimp and Rice

1 small onion, diced
1 bell pepper, chopped
1 tsp. vegetable oil
1 box of rice and beans
1 can of seasoned tomatoes
1 can shrimp
2 cups water
Cayenne and paprika

Saute the onions and pepper in vegetable oil. Add in the remaining ingredients. Simmer in a covered pot for approximately 15 minutes and serve.

Bagged Camp Tacos

Ground beef /chicken
Taco seasoning
Sliced tomatoes
Sliced onions
Shredded cheese
Tortilla chips
Cook the ground beef until there is no sight of pink, drain fat and add taco seasoning. You may have to add a little bit of water to the meat and seasoning mix. Put all ingredients in a large zip-tight then add meat. Shake until mixed. Pour onto tortilla chips or eat out of the bag!

Best Campfire Chili Ever

2 lbs. cooked hamburger/ground chicken
2 jars of salsa
2 large cans hot chili beans
2 cans chopped tomatoes
2 cans of tomato juice
2 pkgs. chili seasoning
Cayenne for added spice
Mix all ingredients together in a large pan and let it cook. This makes a lot of chili. Tip: make this after breakfast and let it sit on the side of the fire and cook all day. Enjoy!

Grilled Camper Potatoes

Large potatoes
Olive oil
Favorite herbs and spices
Cut potatoes into 1/2-inch slices. Brush with olive oil and add favorite herbs and spices if desired. Lay on grill. Sprinkle with salt and pepper to taste. Turn as desired until tender and browned.

Camp Bread

9 cups of regular Quaker Oats
3/4 lb. of butter or margarine
2 cups of white sugar
1/3 cup of corn syrup—clear
1/3 cup of honey
1 tsp. of maple syrup
Raisin or nuts (optional)
Cinnamon

Put 1 cup at a time of oats into the blender or food processor and chop at high speed for a few seconds. Some large flakes should remain. Combine other ingredients in a mixing bowl, and then slowly mix in the chopped oats. By the time all the oats have been added, the mixture will be very thick and stiff, requiring either a heavy duty mixer or some hand mixing with a strong spoon. Place in bread pan and bake in oven until golden brown.

Campfire Onions

1 sweet Vidalia onion
4 strips of bacon
2 tbsp. butter

Quarter the onion (do not cut all the way through). Place strips of bacon crosswise in cut of onion. Wrap in foil with the butter. Place in coals of fire.

Orange-Flavored Gourmet Pork Chops

2/3 cup olive oil
1 cup orange juice
2 tsp. orange peel zest
2 tsp. dried sage
1 clove garlic, peeled and crushed
Salt and pepper
1/4 tsp. of cayenne
4 pork chops, 1-inch thick

Marinade: In large re-sealable plastic bag, mix olive oil, orange juice, orange zest, sage, garlic, salt, pepper, cayenne. Mix well. Remove excess fat and add the chops to the marinade and cover or seal. Place in refrigerator or cooler for 12 to 24 hours.

Heat grill on medium heat. Remove chops from bag and place on grill. Cover grill and cook for 10 minutes, turning over at the five-minute mark. Cut center to determine if center is slightly pink for doneness.

Campfire Sausage and Beans

1 or 2 tbsp. vegetable oil
1 medium-sized onion, thinly sliced
1 medium-sized green pepper, cut into 1/2-inch squares
1 15-oz. can baked pork and beans
1 15 oz. can of butter beans, drained
1 small can sliced mushrooms, drained
5 oz. cooked sausage
1/2 cup of catsup
1/4 cup mustard
2/3 cup maple syrup
1 tsp. oregano
5 whole garlic cloves
2 small bay leaves

Heat the oil in a large saucepan over a low fire. Sauté onion and pepper until the onion is transparent (couple of minutes). Add beans, sliced mushrooms and stir well. Cut the sausage into bite-sized pieces and add together with the catsup, mustard, maple syrup, oregano, garlic cloves and bay leaves. Simmer, stirring occasionally, until all the ingredients are piping hot. Remove bay leaves. Serve immediately.

Campfire Rock Chicken

3–5 softball-sized rocks
2 celery sticks
Medium onion
1 whole chicken
Foil
Newspaper

Place rocks in the campfire so they get very hot. While heating the rocks, clean a whole chicken inside and out and then rub it with salt and pepper for taste. Take two full-sized celery sticks and 1 medium-sized cooking onion and stuff inside the chicken. When rocks are heated and hot, take a pair of sturdy BBQ tongs, pick up one of the rocks and stuff into the chicken with the celery and onion. Then place the chicken on a large sheet of foil and take the other two rocks and place one under each wing.

Now wrap the chicken in foil (the more foil the better but make sure you use a good amount otherwise the rocks can burn through the foil). Now, wet some newspaper and wrap it around the foil chicken. Wrap 10–15 layers. This holds the heat of the rocks in very well. Let sit and cook for about 3 hours.

Lemon Mustard Campfire Trout

4 medium-sized trout
1/2 tsp. salt
1/3 cup milk
1/2 cup flour
1 tbsp. oil
6 tbsp. butter
2 1/2 tsp. of mustard
1 tsp. parsley flakes
2 tbsp. lemon juice

Clean, wash and dry the trout. Combine salt and milk in bowl. Dip each piece of trout in the milk mixture and then roll in a separate bowl of flour. Heat the oil and 3 tbsp. of the butter in a large skillet. Cook the trout until tender and crispy. Remove and keep warm. Quickly add and stir the mustard, leftover butter, and the parsley flakes into the pan. Then add the lemon juice, and bring to a boil. Pour the mixed contents over the fish and serve.

Sweet and Salty Corn on the Cob

8–10 cobs of corn
1/2 cup honey
2 tsp. salt
1/4 cup water

Gently pull the husks down from the corn but do not tear them off and remove the corn silk. Mix the honey, salt and water in a small saucepan, bring to a boil for 3 minutes. Brush the corn with the mixture, then pull the husks up and wrap the opened tops with foil. Place the wrapped corn in the hot coals. Turn frequently for 20 minutes.

Camper's Stew

1 1/2 pounds plain or garlic sausage
1/2 pound cooked chicken
4 tbsp. vegetable oil
4 medium onions, thinly sliced
4 tbsp. flour
1 cup of beef broth
2 cups of cooking wine
3 tbsp. tomato paste
2 cups tomato juice
3 garlic cloves, crushed
2 1/2 pounds sauerkraut, drained
2 large potatoes

Cut the sausage into 1/2-inch slices and the chicken into 1-inch cubes; set aside. Heat the oil in a skillet and sauté the onions until they are golden and transparent. Blend the flour in with the onions. Gradually stir in the broth, cooking wine, tomato paste, tomato juice and garlic. Cook gently, stirring constantly, until the sauce thickens. Remove the sauce from the flame. Rinse the sauerkraut in water and drain well. Peel and slice the potatoes. Layer a large pan with sauerkraut, sausage, chicken, potatoes and sauce to form four layers. Cover and simmer for 2–21/2 hours over low heat or place in a Dutch oven and cook in a pit. Serve hot.

Hash Brown Delight

1 package of cubed or shredded hash browns
1 lb. of diced sausage, bacon, or ham
6 eggs, beaten
1 small onion chopped

1 clove of garlic crushed
Salt and pepper and cayenne for added spice
8 oz. grated or shredded cheese
Spray Dutch oven, skillet or pan with a non-stick spray. Then add hash browns and top with meat. Beat eggs with onion, garlic, salt and pepper; pour over potato/meat mixture and top with cheese. Bake for about 30 minutes. Use catsup for topping.

Camper's Cornbread

1 tsp. salt
3 tbsp. baking powder
3/4 cup cornmeal
1 1/4 cups flour
1 cup milk or water
1 egg, beaten
4 tbsp. sugar
4 tbsp. butter or margarine, melted
1 3/4 cups whole-kernel corn
Mix salt, baking powder, sugar, cornmeal, and flour together. Then add the milk or water, egg, sugar, butter and corn. Mix well and pour into greased Dutch oven. Place 1–2 inches of coals under the Dutch oven and 2–3 inches on top, Bake for approx. 25–45 minutes.

Grilled Cajun Campfire Bass

2–3 lbs. of bass fillets
1/2 cup melted butter
Salt and pepper to taste
1/2 tsp. Cajun spice (cayenne/paprika)
1/4 tsp. onion salt
1/4 tsp. paprika
1/4 tsp. garlic salt
1 lemon
Preheat camp grill or prepare open fire. Lay fillets flat on aluminum foil with an inch or so between. Brush fillets with butter and sprinkle remaining

ingredients evenly over fillets. Wrap fillets in aluminum foil—make sure it's completely sealed. Place foil packet on campfire or grill and cook for 7–10 minutes. Very hot—be careful when opening.

Camp-Style Walleye

2–3 of Walleye fillets
3 tbsp. of butter
Seasoning salt and pepper
Lemon juice
Foil

Put 2–3 fillets on aluminum foil and put a bit of butter on each fillet. Add seasoning salt and pepper and sprinkle fillets with lemon juice. Seal fillets in aluminum foil and grill for 12–15 minutes, or until fish flakes with a fork.

Fried Fisher's Trout

2 cups of milk
Salt and pepper
Cayenne
2 lbs. of fresh trout fillets
1/4 cup flour
1/2 cup butter
3 tbsp. lemon juice
3 tbsp. chopped parsley
Lemon wedges

Season the milk to taste with salt, pepper, and cayenne. Soak the trout in the milk mixture for 5 minutes. Remove the trout and coat with flour. Place the skillet on hot coals and melt the butter in it. Place the trout in the skillet and brown each side. Raise the skillet just above the hot coals using 2 sticks. Cook for 8–10 minutes and sprinkle the trout on both sides with lemon juice and simmer for 30 secs. Sprinkle the trout with the chopped parsley and serve with the lemon wedges on the side.

Grilled Teriyaki Orange Trout

3/4 cup teriyaki glaze or sauce
3/4 tsp. powdered ginger
5 ounces of orange juice
1 tbsp. cilantro, finely chopped
Salt and pepper
6 trout fillets

Mix together teriyaki sauce, ginger, juice, cilantro, salt, and pepper. Brush the trout with sauce mixture and cook over a campfire grill. Cook for 10–12 minutes or until fish flakes with fork.

Cedar Salmon Fillets

Small cedar plank, about 18 in. long x 10 inches wide
2–3 salmon fillets
Italian dressing
Seasoning salt and pepper
Parsley
Spray bottle for water
Zip-tight bags

Soak the cedar plank in water for 30 minutes. Mix together the dressing, salt and pepper, and parsley and place it in zip-tight bag. Then place salmon fillets in bag and marinate for 30 minutes while the board is soaking. You can marinate longer—the longer the board soaks the better. Once the board has finished soaking, remove and place on campfire grill over medium-sized flames. Place salmon fillets on top of cedar board and cook until fish flakes. The board may catch fire, so be sure to have your spray bottle to tame the flames!

Tater Tot Surprise

1 lb. ground beef/chicken/pork
1/2 cup of frozen chopped onions
Salt and pepper
1 can cream of celery soup
1/2 cup desired vegetables

1/4 cup of water

4 cups frozen Tater Tots

Preheat oven to 400°F. Spray a 2-quart baking dish with non-stick spray. Cook ground meat and onions in a skillet over medium heat; drain. Sprinkle with salt and pepper. Add cooked meat and onion to the baking dish, cover with the can of soup as is. Add in desired vegetables and add the water, then layer top with Tater Tots. Bake for 40–45 minutes; the center should bubble.

Cheesy Catsup Camper Meatloaf

1 package of gravy mix

1 lb. of extra-lean ground beef/chicken/pork/turkey

1 green onion, finely chopped

Salt and pepper

2 cups mashed potatoes

1 tsp. chopped chives

1/2 cup of shredded cheese

Catsup

Preheat oven to 350°F. Combine gravy mix with ground meat mixture, onion, pepper, and salt. Pour mixture in a baking pan. Boil and mash potatoes and add a little milk to make them creamy. Add chives to the potatoes, mix and spread over meat mixture.

Place baking pan in oven and cook for 50–60 minutes. When finished cooking sprinkle top with cheese immediately so it melts and stick back in for a couple of minutes, oven still should be hot after you turn it off. Serve with catsup.

Red Pepper Salsa Salmon

Fillet of salmon

Salt and pepper

Parsley

1 tsp. lemon juice

Red Pepper Salsa:

1 cup chopped red peppers

2 medium celery stalks, diced
1/4 cup minced red onion
1 minced jalapeño chili pepper
1/2 cup chopped green onions
1/2 tsp. sugar
1/4 tsp. salt
2 lemon wedges

Clean salmon. Grill salmon in skillet over low heat until it flakes with a fork. Mix salt, pepper, and parsley together with the lemon juice. Prepare salsa in a separate bowl and mix together all ingredients and squeeze lemon wedge juice in salsa mixture. Top salmon with salsa mixture.

Chicken and Veggie Casserole

1 cup instant rice
1 can of cream of mushroom soup
1 can of cream of celery soup
1 cup water
1 cup chopped chicken
1 cup grated carrots
1/4 cup green onions
Salt and black pepper

Preheat oven to 350°F. Cook rice according to directions. Combine soup and water and bring to a boil, then add chicken. When rice is done add it to the soup and chicken mixture. Simmer on low heat for 10–15 minutes. Pour mixture into casserole dish and add in grated carrots, green onion, salt and pepper. Cook for 25–30 minutes.

Chicken a la Mode Camper Style

2 cups bread crumbs
1 tsp. oregano
1 tbsp. parsley
Salt and pepper
1 tbsp. garlic salt
1 tbsp. onion powder

4 egg whites
1 tbsp. skim milk
4 boneless, skinless chicken breasts
Non-stick cooking spray

Preheat oven to 375°F. Wash chicken well. Combine the bread crumbs, oregano, parsley, salt, pepper, garlic salt, and onion powder in a bowl. Combine eggs and milk in separate bowl and coat each piece of chicken with mixture. Dip coated chicken into bread crumb mixture. Spray baking sheet with non-stick spray and bake for 40–45 minutes.

Almond Chicken

2 boneless chicken breasts
1 egg white, lightly beaten
1/4 tsp. allspice
1/4 tsp. ground pepper
1/2 tsp. cayenne
1/2 tsp. crushed chili pepper flakes
1 tbsp. slivered almonds

Preheat oven to 350°F. Clean chicken. Place egg white in bowl. Dip each chicken breast and coat with egg. Sprinkle chicken with allspice, pepper, cayenne, and chili pepper flakes. Coat chicken with slivered almonds. Line a baking dish with foil and coat with cooking spray. Cook for 35–40 minutes until chicken is no longer pink.

Baked Asparagus

2 lbs. of asparagus
1 tbsp. olive oil
1 tbsp. lemon juice
Salt and pepper

Preheat oven to 450°F. Wash asparagus and snap bottoms of stems (white part). Brush asparagus with olive oil. Bake in oven for 20 minutes until tender. Sprinkle lemon juice, salt, and pepper mixture on top of asparagus.

Spiced Cod

2 cod fillets
2 tbsp. of soy sauce
1/2 cup water
2 tbsp. apple cider vinegar
3 tbsp. olive oil
2 tbsp. sweetener
1 tbsp. thyme
2 tsp. chili pepper flakes
2 tsp. allspice
2 tsp. minced onion
1 tsp. paprika
Salt and pepper
Lemon wedges for garnish

Preheat oven to 450°F. Clean cod. Blend other ingredients except salt and pepper together well in a casserole dish. Add cod and marinate for 20 minutes. Remove cod and drain excess marinade from dish. Bake for 20–30 minutes. Add salt and pepper to cooked cod and serve with lemon wedges.

Oriental Chicken Salad

4 boneless skinless chicken breasts
1 cup seasoned rice vinegar
4 tsp. sweetener
2 tbsp. olive oil
Salt and pepper
1 tbsp. ginger
2 tbsp. soy sauce
1/4 tsp. chili pepper
1 large garlic clove
2 tbsp. sesame seeds
2 tbsp. slivered almonds
4 slices of ginger
1 small head of cabbage, thinly sliced
2 cups romaine lettuce
2 green onions, thinly sliced

1 large bell pepper, sliced in thin strips
1/4 cup cilantro
1 shredded carrot
1 cup of mandarin oranges, drained

Clean chicken well. Spray skillet with non-stick cooking spray and cook chicken until no longer pink. When chicken has cooled cut into strips one inch wide. Combine rice vinegar, sweetener, olive oil, pepper, salt, ginger slices, soy sauce, chili pepper, and garlic in large bowl.

Combine sesame seeds, slivered almonds, ginger, cabbage, lettuce, green onions, bell pepper, cilantro, carrot, and mandarin oranges in a separate bowl. Toss dressing into sesame mixture, and serve with chicken.

Taco Salad Supremo

1 lb. of lean ground meat
1 tbsp. chopped onions
1 packet taco seasoning mix
2 tbsp. salsa
1 diced tomato
1 diced jalapeno pepper
2 cups shredded lettuce
Shredded cheese
1 tbsp. of sour cream
1 crushed taco shell

Cook ground meat and onion together and drain fat. Stir in taco seasoning mix and bring to boil. Reduce and simmer for 10 minutes. Mix all ingredients over salad.

Creamy Tuna and Pasta Salad

11/4 cup low-fat mayonnaise
1/2 cup skim milk
2 tbsp. lemon juice
Salt and pepper
1 1/2 tsp. thyme
1 1/2 cup of drained tuna

1 cup grated carrot
1/2 cup chopped onion
3/4 cup diced celery
3 cups of cooked shell pasta
Cook and boil pasta. Combine and mix together mayonnaise, milk, lemon juice, salt, pepper, and thyme. Mix in tuna, carrot, onion, celery and serve over pasta. Refrigerate for cold pasta.

Shrimper's Dill Salad

1 lb. of cooked shrimp, peeled
3/4 cup celery, finely diced
3/4 cup nonfat sour cream
2 1/2 tbsp. lemon juice
2 tbsp. fresh dill
1 1/2 tsp. oregano
Salt and pepper
9 cups mixed salad greens
2 tbsp. olive oil
1 cup cherry tomatoes
Chop cooked shrimp into small pieces and place them in large bowl with diced celery. Combine in separate bowl sour cream, lemon juice, dill, oregano, salt, and pepper. Pour this mixture over the shrimp and celery and mix well. In large separate bowl toss mixed greens with olive oil and a pinch of salt. Mix shrimp mixture with greens. Top with cherry tomatoes.

Spicy Black Bean Tortillas

1 cup of black beans, rinsed and drained
1 jar of salsa
1 1/2 chopped green onion
3 jalapeño, seeded and chopped
5 large eggs
8 corn tortillas, each cut into quarters
Shredded cheese
Preheat oven to 475°F. In a small bowl mash 1/2 cup of black beans until

paste. Spray skillet with a non-stick cooking spray. Heat up salsa, green onion, 1/2 cup of mashed bean paste and remaining whole beans, and jalapeño over high heat. Reduce heat to medium-low and break each egg individually on top of bean mixture. Then cover and simmer for 8–10 minutes. Arrange tortillas on large baking sheets, spread bean mixture inside and bake for 7 minutes until lightly browned. Remove tortillas and top with shredded cheese, stick back in oven until cheese melts and serve.

Strawberry Almond Salad

1 cup slivered almonds
2 cloves garlic, minced
2 tsp. honey
1 tsp. Dijon mustard
1/2 cup raspberry vinaigrette
2 tbsp. balsamic vinegar
2 tbsp. brown sugar
1 cup vegetable oil
1 head romaine lettuce, torn
1 pint fresh strawberries, sliced
1 cup crumbled feta cheese
In a skillet over medium-high heat, smoke the almonds, stirring frequently, until lightly toasted. Remove from heat, and set aside. Combine the dressing by whisking together the garlic, honey, Dijon mustard, raspberry vinaigrette, balsamic vinegar, brown sugar, and vegetable oil in a large bowl. In a separate large bowl toss together the toasted almonds, romaine lettuce, strawberries, and feta cheese. Cover with the dressing mixture, and toss to serve.

Cast Iron Skillet Dinner

4–5 sausages
6 white potatoes, sliced
1 large onion, sliced
2 bell peppers, diced
2 medium yellow squash, sliced

Vegetable oil
Salt and pepper
Garlic powder
Heat oil in large skillet over campfire grill. Cook sausage and remove from heat. Using the same skillet, heat oil, then add sliced potatoes and begin cooking. Add each ingredient separately, then the sausage and cook until potatoes are soft. Best when cooked on a campfire, but works fine on stove.

Garlic Chicken

1 whole chicken, cut up
1 bottle soy sauce
Garlic cloves, pressed and crushed
Salt and pepper
Cayenne
Onion Powder
Press and crush garlic cloves. Take a small knife and poke small holes into the chicken. Insert garlic in all holes. Baste the chicken with the soy sauce and season with salt, pepper, cayenne, and onion powder. Cook on campfire grill until no longer pink.

BBQ Bagged Campfire Chicken

3 lbs. chicken legs, thighs and wings
1 1/2 cup BBQ sauce
1 1/2 tsp. garlic powder
1 can of beer
Salt and pepper
1 1/2 tsp. onion powder
1 tsp. cayenne for spice
Clean and wash chicken well. Combine BBQ sauce, garlic powder, beer, salt and pepper, onion powder, and cayenne in zip-tight bag. Put chicken in bag and place in cooler for a few hours. Remove chicken from bag and cook on fire while basting with left over ingredients.

Roasted Corn on the Cob

Corn on the cob, husks on
Large bucket of water
Cut the silk at end of the corn off, and soak cobs in bucket of water for 25 minutes. Place corn directly on hot coals, turning frequently with tongs. Cook approximately 15–20 minutes. Remove husks and top with butter and salt.

Pineapple, Ham and Potato Foil Pack

Flaked or cubed ham
Canned white potatoes, cut into square bite-size pieces
Canned chunks of pineapple
2 tbsp. of butter
1 tbsp. brown sugar
On square of foil combine ham, bite-size potatoes and chunks of pineapple. Add 2 tbsp. of butter and sprinkle with brown sugar. Seal foil pack and cook over campfire until tender.

Grilled Wine Chicken

2 whole chickens cut into quarters
3/4 cup of cooking wine
2 cups minced shallots
1 cup chopped fresh tarragon
2 tbsp. salt
3 tbsp. sugar
Zip-tight bags
Combine ingredients in a zip-tight bag and add chicken. Marinade for 2 hours and cook over campfire grill until chicken is no longer pink.

Lime Chili Chicken Marinade

1–2 skinless chicken breasts

1/2 cup lime juice
1 tsp. garlic, finely chopped
2 tsp. finely chopped ginger
1 tbsp. soy sauce
1 tsp. red chili, finely chopped
2 green onions, chopped
Zip-tight bags

Clean and wash chicken. Add ingredients together in a zip-tight bag. Add in chicken and marinade for 2–3 hours. Then cook on grill.

Lime Salmon Steaks

2 salmon steaks
1 lemon
1 lime
4 tbsp. butter
1 tbsp. olive oil
Salt and pepper

1 tsp. garlic, minced

1 tsp. cumin

Place salmon steaks on aluminum foil. Grate lemon and lime into zest in a small bowl, blend with butter and set aside. Squeeze both lemon and lime over salmon steaks. Drizzle salmon steaks with olive oil and add salt, pepper, garlic, and cumin. Slice the remaining lemon and lime and lay over salmon. Place the butter zest mixture over each salmon steak. Fold the foil around the salmon steaks. Place foil salmon pouches on campfire grill and cook until the salmon flakes. Be careful to not overcook the salmon steaks, as they are best tender and juicy not well done.

Camping Cream Sauce

1 1/2 cups dry white wine

1 cup heavy cream

4 tbsp. Parmesean cheese

1/4 pound Gorgonzola cheese

Black pepper

In saucepan, cook wine over very high heat until reduced by half. Add cream and let cook for approximately 2 minutes. Reduce heat to medium and add Parmesean, Gorgonzola and pepper. Stir until sauce is well mixed and creamy. Add to favorite cooked pasta and mix. Add grilled chicken if desired, by slicing chicken breasts into strips.

Swiss Cheese Pasta in a Red Pepper Cup

2–4 red peppers

1 small onion

1/2 cup grated Swiss cheese

2–4 servings of pre-cooked sea shell pasta

1 cup evaporated milk

Evenly cut the top off of the peppers, keeping the pepper top to work as a lid when the pepper is stuffed. Chop the onion into very small pieces and grate the Swiss cheese. In a bowl mix the pre-cooked sea shell pasta with the evaporated milk, onion and Swiss cheese. Scoop the pasta mix into the red peppers. Add the pepper top back on top, making a lid for the pepper cup.

Wrap the peppers in tin foil and place them on the campfire cooking rack. Cook the peppers for 10–20 minutes depending on the heat of the fire. If available, dribble a little olive oil over the pepper. When ready, simply remove the pepper top and enjoy! Eat right out of the pepper or cut the pepper open and mix in with the pasta.

Drinks

Lemon-Cranberry Iced Cooler

2 quarts iced tea mix
1 can (6 oz.) frozen cranberry concentrate, thawed
1 cup lemonade
1/4 cup sugar
In large pitcher, combine all ingredients; chill. Serve in ice-filled glasses.

Peanut-Chocolate Shake

1 cup milk
4 ice cubes
2 tbsp. peanut butter
1 scoop chocolate powder
Blend milk and ice, add in peanut butter and chocolate powder and blend. Enjoy!

Fruit Shaker

1 banana
1 cup frozen strawberries
1/2 orange
15 grapes
1 cup milk
1/2 cup cubed pineapples
4 ice cubes
1 scoop vanilla powder
Combine all ingredients in blender and blend until smooth. Enjoy!

Strawberry Apple Shake

1 apple
2 cups milk
3 scoops strawberry ice cream
2 tbsp. white sugar or brown sugar
Peel and core apple. Combine milk, ice cream, and sugar in blender. Blend until smooth. Serve cold.

Banana Shake

2 bananas
1 tbsp. lemon or lime juice
4 tbsp. white sugar
1 cup milk
1 cup plain yogurt
Blend together and enjoy!

Mocha Shake

1 cup French vanilla coffee creamer
4 tsp. instant coffee
2 1/4 cups ice cubes
4 large scoops vanilla/chocolate ice cream
Place vanilla-flavored creamer and instant coffee in blender; cover. Blend until coffee is dissolved. Add ice and ice cream; blend until smooth. Serve immediately.

Vanilla Chocolate Milkshake

3 cups chocolate ice cream
1 cup of vanilla ice cream
2 cups milk
1/4 cup brown sugar
1/4 cup white sugar

1/4 cup ground cinnamon

In a blender, combine ice cream, milk, brown sugar, white sugar and cinnamon. Blend until smooth. Pour into glasses and serve.

Root Beer Supreme Dream

Vanilla ice cream
1 (12 oz.) can of root beer
1/2 cup whipped cream
Cherries

Place 1–2 scoops of ice cream into 2 glasses. Pour root beer over ice cream and top with whipped cream and cherries.

Berry Strawberry Shake

4 ounces strawberries, hulled
1 cup milk
1 tbsp. sugar
6 cubes ice

In a blender, combine ice cubes, strawberries, milk and sugar. Blend until smooth. Pour into glass and enjoy!

Razmatazz Shake

1 1/2 cups raspberry juice
3 scoops raspberry sherbet
1/2 cup carbonated water or raspberry soda

In a blender, combine raspberry juice, raspberry sherbet and carbonated water or soda. Blend until smooth. Pour into glasses and serve.

Orange-Vanilla Mania

1 (6 oz.) can frozen orange juice concentrate
1 cup milk
1 cup cold water
1 pint vanilla ice cream

1/2 cup sugar

1 tsp. vanilla extract

10 cubes ice

Combine all ingredients in a blender. You can replace vanilla ice cream with any flavor you wish. Blend until smooth and thick. Pour and serve.

Cookies and Cream Dream Shake

2–3 scoops cookies and cream ice cream

1 1/2 cups milk

2 tsp. white sugar

In a blender, combine ice cream, milk, and sugar. Blend until smooth. Pour into glasses and serve.

Campers Homemade Hot Chocolate Mix

1 1/2 cup instant dry milk

3 tbsp. powdered creamer

1/2 cup sugar

1/2 tsp. cinnamon

1/3 cup cocoa

Marshmallows

Mix well. Add water to 3 tbsp. of mix and enjoy! Store in an airtight container.

Limenade

6 cup cold water

1/3 cup granulated sugar

3–4 green limes

Mix well and serve.

Apple Lime Punch

4 cups chilled apple juice

2 cups chilled lemonade

2 16oz. carbonated lime drink
1 tsp. lime juice
Mix well. Serve and enjoy!

Coconut Cream Drink

3 tbsp. coconut cream (canned)
Can of pineapple juice
Ice
Combine all ingredients and blend. Serve and enjoy! You can add more coconut cream for an extreme coconut taste.

Caribbean Dream

3/4 cup vanilla frozen yogurt or preferred flavor
3/4 cup pineapple sherbet or any fruit sherbet
3/4 cup tropical fruit salad, canned and drained
1/4 cup frozen banana-orange juice concentrate or preferred fruit juice
1/4 tsp. rum-flavored extract
Place frozen yogurt, sherbet, fruit salad, concentrate and extract in blender. Blend on medium speed 1–2 minutes until smooth and well-blended. Pour into two serving glasses and serve immediately.

Citrus Julius

6 oz. frozen citrus juice concentrate
1 cup cold milk
1 cup cold water
6 ice cubes
2 tbsp. sugar
1 tsp. vanilla extract
Place ingredients in blender and blend until smooth. Pour and enjoy.

Frozen Peach Delight

1 frozen peach, peeled

1 cup ice
1/4 peach yogurt
1/2 cup of milk
Peel and freeze peach for at least 30–45 minutes. Then place all ingredients in blender, blend until smooth, and serve.

Blueberry Limonade

1/3 cup freshly squeezed lemon/lime juice
2 cups water
2 cups fresh blueberries
1/2 cup sugar
Combine lemon/lime juice, water, blueberries and sugar in blender. Blend and enjoy!

Camp Champagne

3 cans of frozen pineapple juice
3 cans of frozen apple juice
1 can frozen lemonade concentrate
3 quarts ginger ale or carbonated lime drink
1/2 cup sugar
Combine all ingredients and freeze mixture overnight.

Fruity Camp Cooler

2 6.5-oz. bottles sparkling water, chilled
1 12-oz. can peach juice chilled
1/2 cup unsweetened orange juice, chilled
1/4 cup unsweetened grapefruit juice, chilled
2 tbsp. lemon juice, chilled
Combine all ingredients. Mix and serve. You can substitute juice with preferred flavors.

Banana Coco Smoothie

2 bananas, frozen
1/2 cup cream of coconut
1 cup milk
1 pint vanilla or chocolate ice cream
2–3 tbsp. of chocolate syrup
Combine and blend all ingredients until smooth. Serve.

Apple Iced Tea

4 black tea bags
1/3 cup honey
3 cups unsweetened apple juice
3 cups boiling water
Lemon slices
Boil tea. Remove bags, add honey and apple juice. Stir well. Pour over ice.

Desserts

Easy Gooey S'mores

Box of graham crackers
Bag of marshmallows
1 container of chocolate icing/frosting
Roast marshmallows till golden brown over campfire. Place a heaping spoonful of chocolate icing/frosting from the container on top of a graham cracker—it's gooey and does not need to melt much. Place roasted marshmallow on top of chocolate and top with another graham cracker.

Personal Pie Iron Pies

2 slices of bread
Preferred flavor pie filling
Butter
Powdered sugar

Butter both slices of bread and place one buttered side down in the pie iron cooker. Add pie filling and place the other slice of bread over pie filling. Cook over fire until bread is browned. Sprinkle cooked pie with powdered sugar.

Campers Apple Crisp

Peeled, sliced apples to fill a Dutch oven or pot halfway
1 1/4 cup flour
1/2 cup quick oats
3/4 cup brown sugar
1 tbsp. cinnamon
3/4 cup butter, melted
Place apples in Dutch oven or large pot. Mix together and combine flour, oats, brown sugar, and cinnamon. Add melted butter to mixture and spread over apples. Cover and bake at approx. 350°F for 40–50 minutes.

Banana Rama

1 banana
1 chocolate bar
4 marshmallows
Chocolate spread or peanut butter (optional)
Peel and slice banana vertically. Then shape foil into the shape of a bowl large enough to fit your Banana Rama. Place a chocolate bar on top of the banana. Add the chocolate spread or peanut butter if you like. Top off with 4 marshmallows. Wrap it tightly in foil and place on coals and cook for 10 minutes. Serve while warm.

Camp Fruit Cake

2 cans of preferred fruit pie filling
1 box of cake mix
1/4 cup water
1/4 cup of milk
Grease a Dutch oven with a non-stick spray, shortening or butter. Mix in the 2 cans of pie filling (your choice of flavor) and then add the cake mix.

Spread evenly throughout Dutch oven. Pour water and milk on top. Cover Dutch oven with lid and put in hot coals. Use a shovel and place some hot coals on top of lid and bake for 25–45 minutes. Test middle of cake with knife to check doneness. If knife pulls out clean it's ready. Let cool for 10–15 minutes when removed from coals.

Sweet Camp Graham Bars

1/2 cup of honey
3/4 cup of butter or margarine
1 tsp. of vanilla extract
2 1/2 cups of grahamflour
1/2 cup flour
1/2 cup of bran or oatmeal
1 tsp. cinnamon
1/2 tsp. baking powder
1/2 cup of water
1/4 cup of milk

Mix and combine together the honey, butter/margarine, and vanilla. Mix well. In a separate bowl combine all dry ingredients and add gradually to the honey, butter and vanilla while adding the water and milk. Mix well.
Using a rolling pin flatten mixture out to approximately 1/2 inch thick. Cut them into rectangular bars with a knife. Place on a baking sheet (no need to grease). Prick them with a toothpick or forks and bake for 15 minutes at 350°F until lightly browned.

Foil Camp Cake and Fruit

3 cans of fruit with syrup
Cake mix + ingredients needed to prepare cake mix
Preheat Dutch oven on fire before preparing the cake and place coals on top of aluminum foil shiny side up. Drain syrup from fruit cans and place in a separate bowl. Pour fruit into Dutch oven. Prepare cake mix as directed but replace water with the fruit syrup. Add cake mix to Dutch oven cover and cook over foiled coals. Cover lid with hot coals make sure coals are evenly spread. Cook for 12–15 minutes, then check to see if done. Let cool before serving.

Coconut Pie Camper Style

1 loaf of sliced French or Italian bread
1 can of sweetened condensed milk
1 bag of flaked sweet coconut
Take a slice of Italian or French bread and dip both sides in a bowl of condensed milk, then dip in a separate bowl of flaked coconut. Place on half a pie iron or roasting fork and roast over the campfire. Coconut will brown when done.

Cinnamon Sugar Biscuits

Refrigerator biscuits
Butter-flavored cooking spray or honey
Cinnamon
Sugar (white or brown)
Flatten refrigerated biscuit on bottom of pie iron and roast over coals until golden brown. Remove from pie iron, spray with butter flavored cooking spray (optional replace w/honey) then roll the cooked biscuit in two separate bowls of cinnamon and sugar.

Delicious Pie Iron Pies

2 pieces of bread (loaf)
Butter-flavored cooking spray
Chocolate spread
Fruit pie filling
Jelly
Peanut butter
Marshmallow
Spray each side of the two slices of bread. Place one on the iron with sprayed side down. Mix together other ingredients, spread on a bread slice and then place other slice with sprayed side out. Place pie iron over coals and cook until toasted. Depending on how hot your fire is, it may take 5–15 minutes.

Campmallow Supreme

Marshmallows
Long stick
Peanuts
Chocolate or butterscotch syrup
Using stick, roast your marshmallow. Pull off stick, then place a couple salted peanuts on top of the marshmallow so they sink inside. Then add a little bit of the chocolate or butterscotch syrup.

Raspberry Cake

2 cups all-purpose flour
1 1/2 tsp. baking powder
1/2 tsp. baking soda
1 tsp. salt
2 tsp. cinnamon
1/2 cup solid shortening
1 1/4 sugar
3 large eggs
3/4 cup buttermilk
1 tsp. vanilla extract
1 cup fresh raspberries

Raspberry Frosting:
1/3 cup butter/margarine
1/2 tsp. salt
3 cups of icing sugar
2 tbsp. of blended raspberries
2–3 tbsp. of milk or cream
1 tsp. vanilla extract
1 tsp. rose water
Preheat oven to 350°F. Blend together the flour, baking powder and soda, salt and cinnamon. Prepare in a separate bowl the shortening and sugar and add the eggs, buttermilk, and vanilla extract. Mix and blend thoroughly. Lastly, add raspberries and mix. Pour into an 8-inch cake pan and bake for 25–30 minutes. Cool. Prepare frosting in large bowl and mix and blend

ingredients well. Frost cooled cake.

Peanutty Butter Cookies

1/3 cup flour
1/4 tsp. baking soda
1/4 tsp. baking powder
1/4 cup butter/margarine
4 tbsp. peanut butter
1 tbsp. brown sugar
1/2 cup granulated sugar
1 egg, beaten
1/4 tsp. nutmeg
1/4 cinnamon

Preheat oven to 375°F. Combine flour, baking soda, and powder in large bowl. Combine margarine and peanut butter in a separate bowl and mix well with spoon until blended. Add sugar and egg and beat well. Combine all dry ingredients and mix well. Scoop tbsp.-size portions onto cookie sheet and flatten with knife or fork. Bake for approx. 8–10 or until golden brown.

Blueberry Rolls

4 egg whites, beaten
1 egg, beaten
2 tbsp. sugar or sweetener
1 cup cottage cheese
3 tbsp. cornstarch
2 tsp. vanilla extract
2 tsp. cinnamon
1 cup fresh or frozen thawed out blueberries
Non-stick cooking spray

Preheat oven to 200°F. In a large bowl, mix together eggs and sugar. Then add in cottage cheese and cornstarch; continue mixing. Stir in vanilla extract and cinnamon. Separate mixture into 4 equal groups and cook each individually for 4–5 minutes in a small pan. Once cooked, place thawed or fresh blueberries on top of wrap. Roll up and enjoy this delicious blueberry treat.

Strawberry-Banana Almond Delight

3 cups sliced strawberries
2 cup of sliced bananas
1/4 cup sugar
1/2 cup of strawberry cream cheese
1 cup cottage cheese
1/4 cup icing sugar
1 tbsp. of water
1 tsp. of milk
1 tsp. of vanilla extract
1/2 cup light whipped cream
3 tbsp. slivered almonds

Blend 2 cups of strawberries and 1 cup of bananas with the sugar in a blender. In a large bowl combine strawberry cream cheese, cottage cheese, icing sugar, water, milk and vanilla extract. In a bowl, scoop 1–2 tbsp. of cheese mixture then add 2–3 tbsp. of the blended strawberries and bananas. Top with light whipped cream and sliced strawberry and banana, and slivered almonds.

Caramel Apple Cinnamon Bars

1/2 cup oil
1/2 cup packed brown sugar
1/2 cup unsweetened applesauce
1 tsp. vanilla extract
3/4 cup caramel syrup
2 cups quick-cooking oats
1/4 cup slivered almonds
1/2 tsp. baking powder
1 tsp. ground cinnamon
Non-stick spray

Preheat oven to 325°F. In a large bowl combine oil, sugar, applesauce, vanilla extract, and caramel. Then add in oats, slivered almonds, baking powder, and cinnamon; mix and blend well. Spray baking pan with non-stick spray and bake for 20 to 25 minutes until golden brown on outside. Cut into rectangular bars and serve.

Fruit Iron Strudels

1 can pie fruit (apples, peaches, cranberries)
Raisins or walnuts
Cinnamon
Sugar
2 sheets puff pastry
Powdered sugar
Cooking spray
Combine and mix fruit in a large bowl with the walnuts, raisins, cinnamon, and sugar. Spray pie iron with non-stick spray. Cut puff pastry sheets into 4 separate and even squares and place a sheet on bottom of pie iron, spoon in fruit mixture. Top with another puff pastry sheet and cook in iron over fire until golden brown.

Chocolate Peanut Butter Melt

Two slices bread
Peanut butter
Pure chocolate
Butter/margarine
Pie iron
Spray pie iron with non-stick cooking spray. Then butter each side of sliced bread. Place one slice butter-side down. Spread peanut butter on both sides that are not buttered. Take a piece of chocolate and place in middle of bread. Cook over fire in pie iron until browned. Delicious!

Camping 4th of July Cake

1 pound cake
1 package of white cake icing
2 pints of strawberries
1 pint of blueberries
Slice your pound cake into 2-inch pieces. Place those pieces on a plate or tray so they form a rectangle in shape. Cover the cake with a thick layer of icing. In the top left corner of the cake, place the blueberries in the icing, making a perfect blue square, just like on the flag. Slice the strawberries in half lengthwise, so they have a flat surface on one side. Place the strawber-

ries in rows, flat side down, to make the cake look like the flag. Remember to keep some room between the rows so that you have even red and white stripes. When done, invite your camp site neighbors over for a happy and healthy 4yh of July celebration!

Sweet Roasted Apples

4 Granny Smith apples
1/2 cup sultanas (not golden raisins)
1/3 cup sugar
1 tsp. ground cinnamon

Remove the cores of apples such that the apples are intact with a tube-like hole right through the center. Keep the skins of the apples. Mix the sugar, raisins and cinnamon together. Stuff the raisin mixture into the cored apples. Compact well and wrap each whole apple in aluminum foil paper to keep all ingredients in place during cooking. Place on embers at campfire, wait 8–10 minutes, remove foil and serve!

Camping Banana Boat

1 banana, unpeeled
Semisweet chocolate chips
Miniature marshmallows
Brown sugar

Slit each banana lengthwise but not all the way through. Leave the skin on (do not peel). Put 1–2 tsp. each of the marshmallows and chocolate chips in slit. Sprinkle lightly with brown sugar. Wrap tightly in foil, being sure to seal ends. Place on grill over campfire or coals, seam side up. Takes about 5 minutes to cook.

Tuna Can Pineapple Cake

2–4 used tuna cans (cleaned thoroughly)
1 package cake mix (eggs and water as required)
1 can pineapple slices (round sections)
1 package icing (ready to serve)

Have a fire ready with flames that are not too high, or move the logs so that there is a section under your campfire grill/rack that does not have high flames. (If the flames are too high and touching the tuna cans, the bottom of the cake will burn.) Lightly grease the cans with butter or margarine if available. Place a full round pineapple slice on the bottom of the can.

Prepare cake mix in bowl according to the package directions. The simpler the cake mix the better. Pour the mix into the tuna cans, filling 2/3 of the can. Place the cans on the campfire cooking rack and cook until the cake has risen and browned on top. Remove from grill when ready and let cool on the picnic table. Top with favorite icing or just enjoy the fresh warm cake without!

Dessert Tacos

1 package of flour tortillas
1 8-ounce package chocolate chips
1 small bag of mini marshmallows
Chocolate syrup, optional
Heat a large frying pan to low to medium heat (non-stick frying pans work the best). Lay one tortilla in the pan. Sprinkle chocolate chips and marshmallows on one side of the tortilla. Fold over the other side of the tortilla to make a taco. Heat for about 30 seconds on each side to start to melt the chocolate chips and marshmallows. Drizzle chocolate syrup over the warm dessert taco when ready for presentation, or any type of topping like caramel, butterscotch, or marshmallow fluff.

Roasted Peach Pecans

Canned peach halves
Mini marshmallows
Brown sugar
Pecans
Tin foil
Take a can of peach halves and put into a tinfoil packet. Add brown sugar and mini marshmallows. Pecans will add a unique texture and flavor. Wrap up your foil packet and place in hot coals until marshmallows are melted. When cooked, you will have delicious syrup and melted marshmallows around your warm peach pecan dessert.

 # Chapter 5: Annual Outdoor Recreation Awards

Family Campground Awards

Amazing Locations

Providence Mountains State Recreation Area—Essex, CA
Devonian Fossil Gorge—Coralville Lake—Iowa City, IA
Goblin Valley State Park, UT
Landsford Canal State Park—Catawba, SC
Watkins Glen—Watkins Glen, NY

Biking Trails

Del Norte Coast Redwoods State Park—Crescent City, CA
Alleghany State Park—Red House Area—Salamanca, NY
South Sandusky Campground—Rend Lake—Benton, IL
Sugar Bottom Mountain—Coralville Lake—Iowa City, IA
Paris Mountain State Park—Greenville, SC

Bird-Watching Spots

Brannan Island State Recreation Area—Rio Vista, CA
Hamlin Beach State Park—Hamlin, NY
Bona Dea Trails System, AR
Landsford Canal State Park—Catawba, SC
Kiptopeke State Park—Cape Charles, VA

Canoeing Spots

Humboldt Redwoods State Park—Weott, CA
Juniper Springs Recreation Area—Ocala National Forest—Silver Springs, FL
Salthouse Branch—Philpott Lake—Bassett, VA
Colleton State Park—Canadys, SC
Palisade State Park—Sterling, UT

Educational and Historical Facilities

Big Basin State Park—Boulder Creek, CA
Wellesley Island State Park—Fineview, NY
SouthEast Alaska Discovery Center—AK
Charles Towne Landing State Historic Site—Charleston, SC
Colonial Dorchester State Historic Site—Summerville, SC

Fishing Spots

Clear Lake State Park—Kelseyville, CA
Selkirk Shores State Park—Pulaski, NY

Crystal Springs Campground—Lake Ouachita—Royal, AR
Enid Lake—Memphis, TN
Leech Lake Recreation Area—Federal Dam, MN
Lithia Springs—Lake Shelbyville—Shelbyville, IL
Devil's Fork State Park—Lake Jocassee—Salem, SC
Kiptopeke State Park—Cape Charles, VA
Lake Wateree State Recreation Area—Winnsboro, SC
Outflow Campground—Youghiogheny River Lake—Confluence, PA

Hiking Trails

Salt Point State Park—Jenner, CA
Harriman State Park—NY
Veterans Trail—Coralville Lake, IA
Kings Mountain State Park—Blacksburg, SC
Warm Springs Recreation Area—Lake Sonoma—Geyserville, CA

Kid-Friendly Parks

California State Railroad Museum—Sacramento, CA
Douthat State Park—Cape Charles, VA
Myrtle Beach State Park—Myrtle Beach, SC
Shoal Bay Campground—Dardanelle Lake, AR
Verona Beach State Park—Verona Beach, NY

Park Beaches

MacKerricher State Park—Mendocino, CA
Fair Haven Beach—Fair Haven, NY
Piney Bay Campground—Dardanelle Lake—London, AR
South Sandusky Campground—Rend Lake—Benton, IL
Yuba Lake State Park—Salt Lake City, UT

Picnic Areas

Devil's Lake State Park—Baraboo, WI

Moreau Lake State Park—Ganesvoort, NY
Oconee State Park—Mountain Rest, SC
Patrick's Point State Park—Trinidad, CA
Pokegama Dam and Recreation Area—Grand Rapids, MN

Romantic Spots

Pfeiffer Big Sur State Park—Big Sur, CA
Devil's Lake State Park—Baraboo, WI
Lake Shelbyville—Shelbyville, IL
Letchworth State Park—Castile, NY
Yosemite National Park—Yosemite, CA

Scenic Views

Mount. Diablo State Park—Clayton, CA
Brady Mountain Campground—Lake Ouachita, AR
Chittenango Falls State Park—Cazenovia, NY
Coral Pink Sand Dunes State Park—Kanab, UT
Lillydale Campground—Dale Hollow Lake—Allons, TN
Massanutten Overlook—Shenandoah River State Park—Warren County, VA
Rose Hill Plantation State Historic Site—Union, SC
Table Rock State Park—Pickens, SC
Warm Springs Recreation Area—Lake Sonoma—Geyserville, CA
Wildwood Campground—Fort Gibson Lake—Fort Gibson, OK

Unique Cabins

Malakoff Diggins State Historic Park—Nevada City, CA
Golden Hill State Park—Barker, NY
Keowee-Toxaway State Natural Area Cabin—Sunset, SC
Malakoff Diggins State Historic Park—Nevada City, CA
Quaking Aspen Cabin—Camp Nelson, CA
The Guillebeau House, Hickory Knob State Resort Park—McCormick, SC

Camping Gear Awards

Top Tents

Criteria based on size, durability, assembly, quality

Eureka!	Twister
Coleman	Montana Big Sky Tent
Sierra Designs	Reverse Combi
Big Agnes	Seedhouse 3
Paha Que	The Perry Mesa

Top Camping Grills

Criteria based on quality, size, efficiency, durability

Coleman   RoadTrip Grill

New River Grill Co.	Stowaway
CobbQ	Cobb Grill
Fridge Xone	FX24 Grill Chill
Sport Grill	Big Gass Grill 2

Top Camping Lighting

Criteria based on quality, durability, design, size.

Brunton	Brunton Liberty Lantern
Coleman	Retro Lantern, full size
Coleman	2D Flashlight (widestream)
Coleman	Remote Control Tent Light
Everlite	Compact Lite
Essential Gear, Inc.	12-LED Lantern
Coleman	Northstar Instastart Propane Lantern

Top Mountain Bikes

Criteria based on handling, design, quality, durability

Mongoose	Rockadile AL
Trek	4300

Specialized	Rockhopper
Giant	Iguana
GT	Avalanche 2.0 Disc

Top Backpacks

Criteria based on size, weight, quality, durability, design

Kelty	Arrowhead 2000
Mountainsmith	Chute
Azora LLC	Camp Mule Pack
Jansport	TT07 X20
Marmot	Vapor 30

Top Canoes/Kayaks

Criteria based on quality, durability, design

Ocean Kayak	Prowler Angler
Old Town	Charles River Royalex

Wenonah	Prospector 15
Bell Canoe Works	Drifter
Innova	Vagabond
Necky Kayaks	Manitou Sport

Top Hiking Boots / Shoes

Criteria based on design, comfort, durability, quality

Lowa	Klondike GTX

HI TEC   Multiterra Mid

Teva	Zakka Mid GTX Hiking Boot
Merrell	Wind River
Montrail	Torre GTX
Asolo	Echo
The North Face	Sierra Mid's
Columbia Sportswear	Titanium Diablo Pass
Nike	Air Tumalo II
Salomon	Extend low

Top Camping Sleeping Bags

Criteria based on quality, durability, design

| Eureka! | Cimarron |
| Slumberjack | Grand Canyon Point Imperial |

Mountain Hardwear	All Mountain Lamina
Sierra Designs	Sun Ribbon/Cloud Ripper
Coleman	Crescent

Top Bug Sprays

Criteria based on quality, effectiveness, scent

3M   Ultrathon Insect Repellent 8
3M   Ultrathon Insect Repellent Cream 12
All Terrain   Herbal Armor Insect Repellent

Sawyer   Family Controlled Release Repellent
Tender Corporation   Ben's
SC Johnson   OFF! Deep Woods

Top Binoculars

Criteria based on the field of vision, focus capability, magnification, size, durability, quality

Brunton   Eterna

Olympus	Magellan WP1
Steiner	Merlin
Nikon	Premier LX
Pentax	DCF MP

Top Digital Cameras

Criteria based on durability, size, performance

Canon	Power Shot SD 500
Panasonic	DMC FX7
Pentax	Optio S5i

Casio	EXZ55
Olympus	Stylus 500

Top GPS Units

Criteria based on size, quality, durability, performance

Navman	iCN 510 Pocket In-Car
Brunton	Atlas GPS

Garmin	GPSMAP 60S
Magellan	Sportrak Topo
Suunto	X9 GPS Watch

Top Pop-Up Campers

Criteria based on size, quality, durability

Starcraft	Starcraft 2106
Viking	Saga 1906 ST

Palomino	Yearling 4103
Jayco	Jay Series 1206
Fleetwood	Victory

Top Fishing Gear

Criteria based on design, quality, performance

Scientific Anglers	Mastery Series Specialty Taper
Stren	MagnaThin fishing Line
Flambeau Outdoors	Sport Soft Satchel Tackle
Minn Kota Motors	Endura and Vector Transom-Mount Trolling
St. Croix	Avid Series AS50ULF Spinning Rod
G. Loomis	SR60102 GL3 Casting Rod
Cabela's	Stowaway 5-Piece / Flywater Fly Combo
Humminbird	SmartCast Fish Finder
Bass Pro Shops	Extreme Lite Baitcast Combo
Shimano	Blackmoon Fishing Backpack

Top Coolers

Criteria based on size, durability, temperature capability, appearance

Coleman   62 Qt Xtreme Wheeled Cooler

Coleman   Green Steel Belted Cooler
Crazy Creek   CoolerRest
Fridge Xone   FX 48 Collapsible with Wheels
Igloo   MaxCold 120

Top Camping Accessories

Unique accessory items that contribute to the overall experience while camping. Characteristics of convenience, uniqueness and quality were considered.

Acorn   Summit Slipper

Coleman	Rechargeable Quick Pump

Coleman	Queen Double High Airbed
Coleman	Camping Coffeemaker
Coleman	Hot Water on Demand

Coleman	Carry Bag (Hot Water on Demand Accessory)
Coleman	Spray Adaptor (Hot Water Demand Accessory)
Coleman	ProCat Heater
Silva	Ranger CL (Compass)
Hydro-Photon	SteriPEN
Benchmade	Rescue Hook

Everlite   Compact Lite
Coghlan's   5 L.E.D. Headlight
Tuga   UV Protection Wear

All Terrain   Outdoor Adventure Kit
Swiss Army   Voyager Lite Ruby Boxed Pocket